C ONTENTS

Part one

Introduction

How to study a novel

Studying a novel on your own requires self-discipline and a carefully thought-out work plan in order to be effective.

- You will need to read the novel more than once. Start by reading it quickly for pleasure, then read it slowly and thoroughly.
- On your second reading make detailed notes on the plot, characters and themes of the novel. Further readings will generate new ideas and help you to memorise the details of the story.
- Some of the characters will develop as the plot unfolds. How do your responses towards them change during the course of the novel?
- Think about how the novel is narrated. From whose point of view are events described?
- A novel may or may not present events chronologically: the time-scheme may be a key to its structure and organisation.
- What part do the settings play in the novel?
- Are words, images or incidents repeated so as to give the work a pattern? Do such patterns help you to understand the novel's themes?
- Identify what styles of language are used in the novel.
- What is the effect of the novel's ending? Is the action completed and closed, or left incomplete and open?
- Does the novel present a moral and just world?
- Cite exact sources for all quotations, whether from the text itself or from critical commentaries. Wherever possible find your own examples from the novel to back up your opinions.
- Always express your ideas in your own words.

This York Note offers an introduction to *Sense and Sensibility* and cannot substitute for close reading of the text and the study of secondary sources.

Sense and Sensibility was the first of Jane Austen's major novels to be published, and shows that her talent for comedy was already well developed, for this is a very funny account of life within a shrewdly observed circle of well-to-do gentry of her day. The humour is to be found in the familiar exercise of her acerbic wit about human nature, as well as in skilfully developed situations, which are likely to make the reader laugh out loud.

There is a large cast of characters, most of whom are related to one another – some closely, some distantly – and, as in every extended family, there is a range of personalities, not all of them demonstrating a kindly nature. Jane Austen has plenty of fun with the pompous, the greedy, the scheming, the hypocritical and the self-deluding among the related Dashwoods, Ferrars, Middletons and Steeles. The narrative centres, however, with more serious purpose – and often with a darker tone – upon the two elder Dashwood girls, Elinor and Marianne; cultivated and with intellectual interests lacking in most of their family, they are also much less prosperous. The natures of the sisters are sharply differentiated by the author at the beginning of the novel and the reader is firmly nudged towards viewing them as personifying the attributes of the title. Elinor demonstrates common sense, a rational approach to events, emotional self-control and a recognition that the rules of society are, on the whole, best observed in everyone's interest. Her younger sister, Marianne, has often been seen as a foil to Elinor's virtues – self-consciously displaying her sensibility through her romantic, individualistic and passionately emotional nature, and not prepared to fall in with society's requirements when they do not suit her.

At first reading, then, it seems that Jane Austen has a straightforward moral purpose in her depiction of the two sisters: to praise balance and moderation (sense) and to deprecate the folly of over-romantic sensibility (a target also in her other novels, particularly *Northanger Abbey*). But the reader becomes less sure of the author's purpose as the story of the sisters' fluctuating fortunes in love unfolds. Certainly, Marianne's exaggerated misery makes her oblivious to the needs of others, but doesn't Elinor's self-control perhaps seem almost so extreme as to be destructive to herself? The reader needs to identify what it is that Austen is telling us about sense and sensibility, and that isn't as straightforward as at first it seems.

Jane Austen is renowned for the wit and polish of her style, but the reader must not be deceived into thinking that nothing much is going on beneath that urbane surface and during the rarely less than polite conversational exchanges. There are often stormy emotions to be recognised, and Austen's dialogue deserves particularly close attention when those who are less than fond of each other are involved: biting malice often lurks in apparently civilised conversation.

Those who have read other works by Jane Austen will find this comedy of manners just as accessible; if this is your first encounter with her novels, don't be surprised to find some sombre notes and hints of tragedy, but above all expect to laugh and to enjoy her wit and comments on human nature, still surprisingly valid at the beginning of the twenty-first century.

PART TWO

SUMMARIES & COMMENTARIES

The text referred to in this Note is the 1995 Penguin Classics edition, edited and introduced by Ros Ballaster.

The first of Jane Austen's novels to appear, *Sense and Sensibility* was published by Thomas Egerton, at the author's expense, in 1811. The first edition, maintaining her anonymity, was advertised at the end of October as 'a New Novel by a Lady' in the *Morning Chronicle* and sold out by the summer of 1813, making £140 for the author. A second edition was published by Thomas Egerton in November 1813, with some alterations, apparently by the author. However, it appears that, although Austen is known to have corrected the proofs of the first edition herself, this was not the case with the second edition, since there are many printer's errors.

While subsequent editors of *Sense and Sensibility* have relied on the second edition, Ros Ballaster has returned to the first edition, which, having been scrutinised by the author, is likely to be more in touch with her original intentions. Textual variations between the first and second editions are noted at the end of the Penguin Classics version.

Today's reader will find punctuation that does not accord with current practice, as well as one or two grammatical usages and some erratic spelling which are Jane Austen's own.

Editions in translation of all Austen's six major novels had appeared in France by the 1820s (including an illustrated *Raison et Sensibilité* in 1828) and in Germany during the 1860s. The key publications in English are, briefly:

> 1833 (reprinted 1866, 1879, 1882): Cheap, one-volume illustrated version in Bentley's Standard Novels series (which included the rest of Austen's published work)

> 1892: A ten-volume edition of Austen's novels, reprinted the same year, published by J.M. Dent and revised in 1966 as the Everyman editions.

1923: R.W. Chapman's scholarly edition of the novels for the Clarendon Press, which has remained the standard authority, still with an emphasis on the 1813 reading.

At the beginning of the twenty-first century, many editions of Jane Austen's work are available, including inexpensive paperbacks and taped readings. The modern reader also has the opportunity to see film and television dramatisations of her work. While even the best of these inevitably lose some of the delights of the text, they nevertheless carefully suggest the settings and dress of which her first readers needed no description but which can be helpful nearly 200 years later.

SYNOPSIS

When Mr Henry Dashwood dies, his wife and three daughters are left without financial security, or even a home of their own. Henry Dashwood's estate passes to John, his son by his first wife. Although John promises his dying father to look after his stepmother and sisters, he is easily persuaded by his greedy wife, Fanny, that he need do nothing for them. John and Fanny move into Norland Park, the Dashwood home. Fanny's brother, Edward Ferrars, and Elinor, the elder Dashwood daughter, spend much time together and are attracted to each other, but generally Mrs Dashwood and her daughters are unhappy in their old home, which is now reigned over by the obnoxious Fanny.

A timely invitation from Sir John Middleton, Mrs Henry Dashwood's cousin, provides them with a small house at a low rent on his estate in Devonshire. Sorry to say a permanent goodbye to their old home (and Elinor particularly sad to say goodbye to Edward), they are nevertheless soon contentedly settled in Barton Cottage.

The Middletons and Sir John's mother-in-law, Mrs Jennings, are hospitable people, although lacking in the cultural interests that occupy the Dashwoods, and many social activities take place at Barton Park. Elinor and her younger sister, Marianne, are much in demand. A great friend of Sir John's, thirty-five-year-old Colonel Brandon, feels himself very much drawn towards Marianne, who dismisses him as impossibly ancient.

The autumn countryside is very beautiful and the Dashwoods enjoy walking in the hills around their house. One day Marianne and her young sister, Margaret, go out rather rashly on a day of uncertain weather. In a rush for home when it begins to rain, Marianne falls, hurting her ankle, and is rescued by the dashing Willoughby. He is handsome and attentive to Marianne and she is soon very openly in love with him. He, too, makes everyone believe that marriage is in the offing, but no engagement is announced. One day he suddenly departs for London, leaving Marianne distraught, although sure of hearing from him soon.

Edward Ferrars pays a visit to Barton Cottage. All the Dashwoods are pleased to see him, although his low spirits and his uneasiness with Elinor upset her. She believes that they love each other, however, and is deeply hurt when she learns that he has been engaged to be married to a distant relation of the Middletons, Lucy Steele, for four years. Foolish Anne Steele and her pretty sister Lucy are a sycophantic pair who are staying at Barton Park; the spiteful Lucy, discovering Elinor's attachment to Edward, enjoys tormenting her with tales of romance under the pretext of seeking Elinor's advice, and requiring the secret of her engagement to be kept. Volume I ends with both Marianne and Elinor suffering for love, although Elinor's self-control is in sharp contrast to Marianne's exaggeratedly emotional behaviour.

Elinor and Marianne are persuaded to accept an invitation from Mrs Jennings to spend some time with her in London. Marianne, who has heard nothing from Willoughby since he left, looks forward to meeting him there. However, he does not respond to her notes, is distant and barely polite when they meet at a party and finally sends her an insolently cruel letter, informing her that he is to be married to the wealthy Miss Grey.

Marianne, whose love for the scoundrelly Willoughby has never faltered, is in a state of collapse, making no attempt to hide her distress from the world. Elinor, also suffering, but silently, supports her sister loyally and eventually Marianne begins to recover. Meanwhile, the Steeles have wormed their way into favour with Edward's snobbish mother, Mrs Ferrars, who is prepared to make a favourite of Lucy in order to snub Elinor, whose fondness for Edward she suspects. In order to avoid having John's sisters to stay, Fanny and John Dashwood have invited the Steeles to their London house. Volume II ends with

Marianne making some attempt to come to terms with her grief, although still very self-absorbed, and Elinor in a state of suppressed wretchedness, having been pledged to silence about Lucy's engagement to Edward.

Volume III opens with high drama: silly Anne Steele, seeing her sister to be apparently such a favourite with Edward's mother and the Middletons, reveals the engagement with Edward. The snobbish and mercenary Middletons throw the penniless Steeles out of their house, Fanny claims to be ill from the shock, and Mrs Ferrars says she will cut off Edward's inheritance unless he renounces the misalliance. Edward determines to honour his engagement and Mrs Ferrars makes her younger and favourite son, the foppish Robert, her heir.

Now that the secret is out, Marianne understands what her sister has been through during the past weeks and recognises her own selfishness. Willoughby is married to his heiress. The girls leave with Mrs Jennings for the home in Somerset of her younger daughter, Mrs Palmer, a step on their way to Devonshire. Marianne, still pensive and solitary, enjoys the Palmers' gardens after the constraints of London, but catches a chill and becomes gravely ill. Colonel Brandon, also visiting the Palmers, goes to fetch Mrs Dashwood from Barton Cottage.

While awaiting her mother, Elinor is astonished to be visited by Willoughby. He has travelled hard on hearing that Marianne is dying, in order to express his repentance and offer some sort of explanation for his behaviour. Colonel Brandon has already told Elinor that he has fought a duel with Willoughby, who has seduced, made pregnant and abandoned the Colonel's ward Eliza, the illegitimate daughter of his dead lost love, who resembled Marianne in looks and temperament. Willoughby's grief and desire to explain bring Elinor to the point of forgiving him, although she recognises that his charm plays a part in this. He did not realise that Eliza was pregnant, it appears, or that she was unable to contact him. He still loves Marianne as he always did, but has made a loveless marriage in order to recoup the losses his extravagance has caused him.

Mrs Dashwood and Colonel Brandon arrive in a state of high anxiety about Marianne, and there is great rejoicing when she is found to be out of danger, although still weak. Colonel Brandon has confided in Mrs Dashwood on the journey and she encourages his love for her daughter.

Back at home in Barton Cottage, the Dashwoods begin to resume the occupations of their normal life, although both Elinor and Marianne are still unhappy. Elinor, who has always believed that she and Edward love each other, in spite of his ill-judged engagement to Lucy, has to give up her last hope when a servant returns from Exeter to announce that Mr Ferrars is married and he has seen him and Lucy Steele in the town. It is almost more than Elinor can bear when Edward arrives on horseback later that day and reveals that he is free: Lucy has broken her engagement to him and married his wealthier brother Robert. Although even the deepest grief never caused Elinor to lose self-control, extreme joy does. When Edward and Elinor have both recovered to some extent, he proposes to her.

Edward, ordained as a clergyman, is offered a living by Colonel Brandon and, with some mean-spirited financial assistance from Mrs Ferrars, is able to marry Elinor and they move into the parsonage on Colonel Brandon's estate at Delaford. Eventually Marianne recovers from her misery over Willoughby's betrayal and marries Colonel Brandon. Unlike the quarrelsome relationships of the John Dashwoods and the Robert Ferrars, the marriages of Elinor and Marianne are happy and harmonious, and the sisters' lives continue to be entwined as they live close to each other.

VOLUME I

CHAPTER 1 (VOLUME I, CHAPTER i)

The Dashwood inheritance

Mr Henry Dashwood, his second wife and three daughters live with Mr Dashwood's wealthy uncle on the latter's estate, Norland Park, in Sussex. On the death of the old uncle, the estate is left to his nephew, Henry, as expected, but is to go upon the death of Henry to the son of his first marriage, John Dashwood, and his male descendants. John has married a wealthy wife and needs the inheritance less than Henry's three daughters, Elinor, Marianne and Margaret. Henry is worried on their behalf and, when mortally ill, asks his son John to promise to look after his stepmother and half-sisters. John's promise is given and he forms the intention of settling £1,000 – a useful sum at the time – upon each of his sisters.

To the dismay of the widowed Mrs Dashwood, her late husband's son, his small boy and his unlikeable wife move into Norland Park without warning as soon as the funeral has taken place. The insensitivity of Fanny's behaviour makes the older Mrs Dashwood want to leave Norland at once. The advice of her more prudent older daughter, Elinor, however, prevails and she reluctantly agrees to stay on to avoid a breach between her girls and their half-brother.

> The dying Mr Henry Dashwood's anxieties about the financial security of his second wife and three daughters would have seemed very real to Jane Austen's readers. The plight of the widow and her three girls, displaced in what had always been their home by the detested Fanny, wins sympathy for them, and their characters are already outlined in this first chapter. Their mother is an emotional and impulsive woman, like her middle daughter, Marianne. Elinor, however, although just as warm-hearted, is able to demonstrate a steadiness of judgement, which is lacking in her impetuous sister, and to control her feelings. Already, in fact, the sense of Elinor and the sensibility of Marianne – and her mother – are sketched in. Margaret, the thirteen-year-old youngest daughter, is mentioned briefly as a good-natured child: she shares some of Marianne's excessive sensibility, but so far lacks her better qualities.

moiety half – not necessarily an equal half
mother-in-law the older Mrs Dashwood is John Dashwood's stepmother in modern terms, rather than his mother-in-law, who for present readers would be Fanny's mother

CHAPTER 2 (VOLUME I, CHAPTER ii)

Fanny's advice

The selfishness of the new owners of Norland Park becomes yet more evident. The scope of John Dashwood's original plan to offer financial assistance to his stepmother and sisters is gradually whittled down, as Fanny reminds him that anything he gives to his 'half blood' (p. 8) relatives will be taken away from his son's eventual inheritance. She reassures him that his father's request that he look after his stepmother and family must have been intended to apply very generally to any assistance John might give them of a non-financial kind. In the end, far from settling money on the girls, or offering an annuity to their mother, John is persuaded that it will be sufficient to help them move to a small house and send them an occasional gift of game from his estate.

John Dashwood is very easily turned from his charitable intentions by his wife, upon whose advice he appears to depend. Fanny, although perfectly polite to her husband's step-relatives, is cold-hearted and clearly greedy: she begrudges them even a set of breakfast china, which belongs to Mrs Dashwood senior.

her life cannot be worth half that purchase John Dashwood believes that his stepmother will not live another fifteen years, and that would reduce the outlay on an annuity

CHAPTER 3 (VOLUME I, CHAPTER iii)

Two views of Edward Ferrars

Six months later, the older Mrs Dashwood and the girls are still living at Norland. Although Mrs Dashwood finds it very irksome to live with Fanny, she still believes that her stepson intends to provide financially for her family. She is also anxious to encourage a growing affection between her eldest daughter, Elinor, and Fanny's brother, Edward, who spends most of his time at Norland. Elinor appreciates his qualities, which are not obvious to Marianne, who finds him lacking in charisma; nevertheless, the younger girl jumps to the conclusion that an engagement is certain.

The marked differences in the characters of Elinor and Marianne are underlined in this chapter. Elinor recognises Edward's worth through her deeper understanding of his nature; Marianne looks for spirit and sparkle, which she finds lacking. She forms her judgement of him on matters such as the fact that he is not a connoisseur of music or drawing, and that he reads aloud in a style she considers dull. (Reading aloud was a familiar domestic evening entertainment of the time.)

Cowper, William an English poet (1731–1800), whose constant theme was human isolation and helplessness. He was a favourite poet of Jane Austen, as he is here of Marianne, even though this character's taste for the exaggeratedly **picturesque** is satirised in *Sense and Sensibility*

CHAPTER 4 (VOLUME I, CHAPTER iv)

A timely offer

In spite of the level-headed Elinor's denials, Marianne and her mother, observing Elinor and Edward together, become ever more convinced that they are engaged to be married, or shortly to be so. Fanny, too, becomes perturbed at their closeness; she anticipates a prosperous match for her brother and considers Elinor quite unsuitable as a future sister-in-law. She intimates as much to Mrs Dashwood, who is deeply offended by the implication that she and her daughters are the social inferiors of Fanny, and that Elinor is trying to ensnare Edward. Mrs Dashwood determines to leave Norland as soon as she can, and is delighted to receive a cordial letter from a relative of hers, Sir John Middleton, who lives on his estate, Barton Park, in Devonshire. Sir John offers his cousin and her girls a nearby property, which he believes may be suitable for them, and for which he asks a nominal rent.

Sir John Middleton's warm-heartedness contrasts strongly with the coldness of Fanny and John Dashwood.

both letters it seems that Mrs Dashwood finds it necessary to send two letters in reply to her cousin, Sir John – perhaps one thanking him for his kindness, and another, more formal, accepting his offer

CHAPTER 5 (VOLUME I, CHAPTER v)

The departure from Norland

Mrs Dashwood takes great pleasure in announcing her impending removal to her stepson and his cold-hearted wife. They are surprised, and Edward Ferrars obviously dismayed, that the new home is to be so far away. Mrs Dashwood makes a polite gesture in inviting John and Fanny to visit them, showing a contrasting warmth, however, when she presses Edward to come and stay as soon as possible.

CHAPTER 5 continued

Within a few weeks, Mrs Dashwood arranges to sell some of her property, including her carriage, and to have the rest of her belongings sent to Devon. Elinor persuades her that three servants will be quite enough in their new home, and two are sent ahead to prepare the cottage for its new tenants.

John Dashwood decides against offering to pay for his stepmother's removal costs, since she is going further than he expected, and she ruefully concludes that he has no intention of making any financial contribution from his father's estate to her or her daughters.

> There are tears as Mrs Dashwood and her daughters leave their familiar home, Marianne in particular demonstrating her exaggerated sensibility as she bids a melancholy farewell to the house and the trees that surround it.

sent round by water it appears that the sea route from Sussex to Devon is preferred to an overland journey for the removal of Mrs Dashwood's belongings

CHAPTER 6 (VOLUME I, CHAPTER vi)

A new home at Barton Cottage

Unhappy at leaving Norland, the girls are nevertheless excited as they approach Barton Cottage. Set in a pleasant valley, and first seen in its autumn landscape, the 'cottage' is in fact a modern and quite substantial building; Mrs Dashwood immediately begins to make extravagant plans for improvements, but the girls are content with their new home. Their landlord, Mrs Dashwood's cousin, Sir John Middleton, is welcoming and generous, with immediate gifts of produce and game, and cordial invitations to his house at Barton Park. Lady Middleton calls on the newcomers as well, with one of her children, but is more reserved than her husband.

> Sir John's treatment of his relatives shows a great contrast to that of John Dashwood, although his wife, Lady Middleton, appears to share some of the self-absorption and chilliness of Fanny Dashwood.

its demesne in front the house has a small, green front garden, presumably laid to lawn

his newspaper newspapers were often shared at a time when they were relatively expensive. Two local daily newspapers are known to have been published in Exeter during the period in which the novel is set

CHAPTER 7 (VOLUME I, CHAPTER vii)

New friends

The Dashwoods make their first visit to Barton Park. Sir John and his wife like plenty of company in their grand house, but on this occasion they have with them only Mrs Jennings, the mother of Lady Middleton, and Colonel Brandon, a friend of their host. Sir John apologises for his failure in being able to produce at short notice any young men to entertain the girls. Those present do not share the Dashwoods' wider cultural interests: the cold-mannered Lady Middleton is absorbed by domestic organisation and her badly behaved children, whom she overindulges; her mother is a noisy and rather vulgar woman – very unlike her daughter – but a cheerful person who gets on well with her son-in-law, Sir John, a typical country squire, whose great love is hunting; Colonel Brandon is a quiet man, an 'absolute old bachelor' (p. 30) in the view of Marianne and Margaret, at the age of thirty-five.

During the evening, the musically gifted Marianne is asked to play. In spite of their rapturous praise, the Middletons are clearly unappreciative – talking during her playing, and asking her to sing a song she has just finished. Colonel Brandon, however, gains merit in Marianne's eyes by his being able – in spite of his supposed great age – to respond to her music-making with sincerity.

Mrs Jennings and Colonel Brandon are to play major parts as the narrative unfolds. Mrs Jennings, however, is seen here as a far from attractive figure, and Colonel Brandon's gravity makes him uninteresting to the younger girls, although his appreciation of music links him to the Dashwoods' interests.

it was moonlight this indicates that it was a busy time socially, since moonlit nights were preferred for evening engagements in the country, as it was easier to see the way home by carriage on the bad and unlit roads

the instrument was unlocked the domestic pianoforte at this time was probably shaped like a harpsichord. That it had to be unlocked suggests that it was a valued item or, perhaps here, that it was rarely used

CHAPTER 8 (VOLUME I, CHAPTER viii)

Some views on marriage

Mrs Jennings, having seen her own two daughters married, enjoys trying to matchmake for others. She believes every pretty girl deserves a good husband, and begins to plan a marriage between Marianne and Colonel Brandon. This would be an ideal match, in her eyes, because '*he* was rich, and *she* was handsome' (p. 32).

After being teased by Mrs Jennings about Colonel Brandon's supposed intentions, Marianne explains her own views on marriage. She believes romantically in young love, seeing Colonel Brandon, whom she has heard complaining of rheumatism, to be so elderly as to be beyond thoughts of marriage. Her sister, Elinor, agrees that perhaps a wife of seventeen – Marianne's age – might be inappropriate for a man of thirty-five, but a woman of twenty-seven or so might well accept him. Marianne gives her opinion that a woman as old as twenty-seven 'can never hope to feel or inspire affection again' and that such a marriage would seem only 'a commercial exchange' (p. 33).

Later, Marianne shares with her mother her anxiety on Elinor's behalf that Edward Ferrars has not yet visited Barton Cottage, although they have been in residence for a fortnight.

Marianne's immaturity is very obvious here. Not only does she have naïve ideas about love and marriage, but she is also unable to understand how her sister Elinor is able to maintain an even temperament and self-control in the face of disappointment over Edward Ferrars' neglect, or of distress at leaving their old home.

an ample jointure Mrs Jennings has had a generous income settled upon her for life, presumably by the terms of her husband's will

CHAPTER 9 (VOLUME I, CHAPTER ix)

Enter Willoughby

The Dashwoods enjoy their usual occupations in their new home, as well as walking in the hilly Devonshire countryside, although the wet autumn weather sometimes keeps them indoors. One morning Marianne and Margaret set out, in spite of a warning sky, and have not gone very far when heavy rain begins to fall. Running for home down a steep slope, Marianne trips and wrenches her ankle. A young man, out with his gun, is nearby and gallantly carries her home. The Dashwoods are charmed by the handsome Willoughby and, when Sir John calls, ask about him. Sir John approves strongly of Willoughby as a sportsman and generally lively young visitor to the area. He is staying at nearby Allenham Court, the owner of which is a relative to whom he is heir.

> Life is agreeable at Barton Cottage, where the Dashwoods take up again their 'ordinary pursuits' (p. 36), which surprises Sir John; he is not used to seeing women reading, making music, drawing or embroidering. The Dashwoods' cultivated activities and discussion of, for instance, aesthetic theories of the **picturesque** set them apart from most of the other female characters in the novel, whose interests are more mundane and domestic.

Mr Willoughby had no property of his own in the country the modern reader understands 'county' rather than 'country', since Willoughby does have a small country estate elsewhere

setting your cap at showing favouritism to an admirer or trying to attract a possible spouse. Women often wore light, sometimes lacy caps indoors, and naturally a young woman would wear her most becoming cap when a hoped-for suitor was at hand

CHAPTER 10 (VOLUME I, CHAPTER X)

Marianne's admirers

Both the older Dashwood girls are attractive, and Marianne especially so. She is a spirited girl, impulsive and frank in conversation. Captivated, Willoughby calls frequently, and Elinor teases her sister about what already seems a close friendship. Marianne finds that her new admirer shares her views on many subjects, including her belief that Colonel Brandon is a dull man. Elinor realises that Colonel Brandon is in love with Marianne and feels sorry for him, since he cannot compete with the sparkling Willoughby.

As so often, the contrast between Elinor and Marianne is most marked by their different views of people. Marianne is in a state of high excitement and interested only in what Willoughby does and says. Elinor notices the unhappiness of Colonel Brandon and speaks up for his qualities, including his 'amiable heart' (p. 45).

Miss Dashwood social convention dictated that only the eldest daughter would be known by her surname; hence, Elinor is known as Miss Dashwood, her sisters as Miss Marianne and Miss Margaret. Similarly, later in the novel, Anne Steele is Miss Steele and her younger sister is Miss Lucy

Cowper and Scott...Pope these writers represent opposite aesthetic poles to Marianne: she admires William Cowper (1731–1800) and Sir Walter Scott (1771–1832), who were key figures in the **Romantic** movement, whereas the earlier Augustan poet Alexander Pope (1688–1744) appeals considerably less. The contrast is between the Romantic writers' expression of emotions, as opposed to the more intellectual and balanced approach of the Augustans

nabobs, gold mohrs, and palanquins colonials returning from India with a large fortune were called 'nabobs', a corruption of the Urdu word for a government official; mohrs were the main gold coins in British India; palanquins were elaborately decorated covered litters, often used to carry dignitaries on state occasions. Willoughby is implying that Colonel Brandon had only mercenary motives for being in India

the hanging of my curricle a curricle was a light, open carriage, usually two-wheeled and drawn by two horses abreast; Colonel Brandon does not approve of the positioning of the body of the conveyance in relation to its axle

CHAPTER 11 (VOLUME I, CHAPTER xi)

Marianne in love

Marianne is clearly falling in love with Willoughby, and makes no pretence otherwise; they are engrossed in each other. Others are less happy: Elinor misses Edward Ferrars and finds the conversation of their neighbours tedious, although Mrs Jennings has become very fond of her. She feels sympathy with poor Colonel Brandon in his apparently hopeless feelings for her sister. He discusses 'second attachments' (p. 49) with Elinor, having discovered that Marianne believes a second love to be impossible. Elinor guesses that he has a tragic romance in his background.

CHAPTER 12 (VOLUME I, CHAPTER xii)

The courtship continues

Willoughby offers a present of a horse to Marianne, but Elinor makes her realise that the expense involved means that she must refuse. Willoughby and Marianne are so much together, and so obviously in love, that her family believes they must be engaged to be married. Margaret has seen Willoughby cutting a lock of Marianne's hair as a keepsake, and reasonably interprets this and their whispering together as confirmation of an engagement, but nothing is said by either of them.

Elinor is teased about her romantic inclinations at Barton Place, but Colonel Brandon tactfully helps to divert those present from the subject. He has organised a visit for them all on the next day to an interesting estate twelve miles away, where a water party is planned.

Although the Dashwoods feel a lack of intellectual and artistic stimulation among their new friends, many entertainments and outings are offered – informal balls, water parties, picnics and dinner parties have already been mentioned.

Queen Mab a magical fairy figure, who brings dreamlike delight. She is mentioned by Mercutio in Shakespeare's *Romeo and Juliet*, and the mare's name is a compliment to Marianne's charm

CHAPTER 13 (VOLUME I, CHAPTER xiii)

Colonel Brandon's mysterious departure

The Dashwoods join the Middleton party at Barton Place for breakfast before the proposed outing, but although the weather is more promising than had been expected, a letter that arrives for Colonel Brandon forces a cancellation. He leaves the table looking disturbed and returns shortly to say he has been called urgently to London. In spite of Mrs Jennings' open curiosity, he reveals nothing further before he departs, offering many apologies for spoiling the outing, which – without his presence – cannot go ahead. He is unable to say when he will return. Mrs Jennings gossips about Colonel Brandon's personal life, shocking Lady Middleton by claiming that he has an illegitimate daughter.

A large party gathers for dinner in the afternoon followed by an evening dance to make up for the lost enjoyment of the day. Marianne and Willoughby go for a drive. Elinor is scandalised to discover, through Mrs Jennings' inquisitiveness, that Marianne has been taken to Mrs Smith's house at Allenham and that Willoughby has shown her over his relative's house and grounds.

> The tragedy or mystery of Colonel Brandon's past, already hinted at in his conversation with Elinor in Chapter 11, looms large here, preparing the reader for subsequent revelations.
>
> Elinor's good sense is demonstrated in her judgement that it was very indiscreet of Marianne to tour the house and gardens of Allenham, when she was unacquainted with its owner and alone with Willoughby. The reader, though, feels some sympathy with Marianne's excitement at a visit to what she obviously believes will be her future home.

> **go post** travel by means of a carriage and relays of horses: this was then the fastest method of travel and indicates that the Colonel is in a hurry
>
> **as like him as she can stare** this nineteenth-century colloquialism means 'very much like him'. To stare did not have the impolite connotations that it has today

CHAPTER 14 (VOLUME I, CHAPTER xiv)

Still no engagement?

While Mrs Jennings continues to wonder what it was that called away Colonel Brandon so urgently, Elinor wonders why her sister has not announced the engagement that everyone expects. Willoughby is clearly in love with Marianne, and his affection extends to Barton Cottage, as he pleads with Mrs Dashwood never to alter it, as she often plans to do.

Jane Austen builds up the reader's expectations of an engagement announcement by the warm exchange between Willoughby and Mrs Dashwood at the end of the chapter, concluding with dinner arrangements for the next day.

CHAPTER 15 (VOLUME I, CHAPTER XV)

A changed Willoughby

Next day, when Mrs Dashwood, Elinor and Margaret return home for dinner after calling at Barton Place, they are not surprised to find Willoughby already there. But Marianne runs upstairs in tears and Willoughby's manner shows a marked change from the ease and affection of the previous day. He explains in some confusion that he has to go away and does not expect to return to the country until the following year. Elinor and her mother are devastated, but Mrs Dashwood soon believes that she has worked out what has happened: she suspects that Willoughby's relative has learned of his attachment to Marianne and is putting pressure on him to go away. Elinor hopes this is the case. Marianne, distraught and unable to eat or speak, offers no explanation.

> This is a second mysterious departure, which is only finally explained towards the end of the novel, revealing a connection between Colonel Brandon and Willoughby. Elinor thinks that Marianne's nature will require her to give exaggerated vent to her grief – and she is right – but, even so, she feels very sorry for her sister.

CHAPTER 16 (VOLUME I, CHAPTER XVi)

A visit from Edward

Marianne's violent grief settles into a quieter state of melancholy after a few days. In spite of Elinor's urging, Mrs Dashwood's delicacy prevents her from asking Marianne if she is indeed engaged to Willoughby, but Marianne reveals that she expects a visit from him soon.

However, the next gentleman visitor disappoints Marianne, since it is not Willoughby but Edward Ferrars. Elinor, too, is disappointed by the long-awaited visit from Edward, to whom she is greatly attached. His manner is awkward and lacks the warmth she would have hoped for. She is surprised, too, that he has already been in Devonshire for a fortnight before making his visit to Barton Cottage.

Marianne's wallowing in grief is seen by the reader as exaggerated, particularly when it appears that she expects soon to be in contact again with Willoughby.

By contrast, Elinor makes an effort to put aside her vexation and disappointment at Edward's chilly behaviour.

nice fastidious. The debased use of the word 'nice' to mean merely agreeable or pleasant is deplored by Henry Tilney in Austen's *Northanger Abbey*

never finished Hamlet reading aloud was a favourite evening pastime among genteel families. (See Part Three: Characterisation for a comment on the play's relationship to Willoughby)

these bottoms must be dirty in winter low-lying parts of the landscape accumulate water in winter and therefore become muddy

CHAPTER **17** (VOLUME I, CHAPTER xvii)

Edward is dull

Mrs Dashwood's charm, often evident in the novel, is explicit here, as she softens Edward's reserve, but he is not in good spirits. A fireside discussion one evening reveals the different approaches to life of the two sisters: Marianne asks, 'What have wealth grandeur to do with appiness?' (p. 80), although it is clear she believes that life would be unendurable without a big house, horses, carriages and servants. Elinor recognises that it is hard to be happy without money, but has much less extravagant ideas of what might be needed for a happy life. Edward joins in the discussion about how all the Dashwoods would spend 'a large fortune apiece' (p. 80). He is surprised and disturbed when Marianne accuses him of being reserved.

Thomson, James English poet (1700–48), whose lengthy work, *The Seasons,* expressed his delight in nature in a way that links him with the later **Romantic** poets

admire an old twisted tree Edward does not share Marianne's enthusiasm for the **picturesque**. (See Part Five: Literary Background for a discussion of the contemporary passion for the picturesque)

CHAPTER 18 (VOLUME I, CHAPTER xviii)

Edward's ring

Edward's reserved manner continues, and he takes care not to be alone with Elinor. He has some fun with Marianne, teasing her about her taste for the picturesque in landscape, as laid down by aesthetic authorities of the era, and demonstrating his own preference for a less emotional response to the beauties of nature.

Marianne notices that Edward is wearing an unfamiliar ring with plaited hair in its centre, and asks if it is his sister's. Edward agrees that it is Fanny's, but appears embarrassed. When he catches Elinor's eye, she is happy to believe that the hair is her own, secretly snipped at Norland without her knowledge.

With the help of Margaret, Sir John and the ever-inquisitive Mrs Jennings identify Edward as Elinor's suspected lover from Norland, and Edward discovers the name of Marianne's beloved.

Elinor is cheered by the belief that Edward is wearing a ring containing a lock of her hair. She prepares herself for future teasing about her supposed romance from Mrs Jennings, whose romantic speculations accompany all developments in the sisters' lives.

banditti Italian robbers or outlaws, who often featured in popular novels, particularly of the **Gothic** genre; they also appeared in **Romantic** landscape paintings of the period

CHAPTER 19 (VOLUME I, CHAPTER xix)

Edward leaves; the Palmers arrive

Edward cannot be persuaded to stay longer than a week, sighs over leaving, and yet has no real reason for departing so soon. He is clearly not a happy man, and at the final breakfast Mrs Dashwood suggests that life would be more agreeable to him if he followed a profession. He explains why he has not done so and states deprecatingly that he has been 'properly idle' (p. 89) since leaving Oxford University. His despondency adds to Elinor's misery at his departure, although she keeps her grief to herself.

A few days later, the Middletons and Mrs Jennings call, bringing with them Mrs Jennings's other daughter, Charlotte, and her husband, Mr Palmer. Mrs Palmer is pregnant and vacuous, if cheerful; her husband tends to silence and irritation. Elinor and Marianne do not look forward to spending the next day with them all at Barton Park.

> There is a great contrast between the extravagance of Marianne's emotions at the departure of Willoughby and Elinor's restraint when Edward leaves. Marianne does not appreciate her sister's self-control and sense, any more than Elinor admired Marianne's demonstrations of extreme sensibility. None the less, Elinor recognised and felt for the other's unhappiness in a way that the more self-centred Marianne is unable to do.

the navy boys began their training in the navy between the ages of twelve and fifteen, so Edward was too old to enlist at eighteen. (Two of Jane Austen's brothers were naval recruits)

red coat an army uniform

Columella reference to the novel *Columella, or, the Distressed Anchoret* (1779) by Richard Graves (1715–1804), based on the life of his friend, William Shenstone, poet and landscape gardener. Columella plans busy lives for his sons, believing that idleness leads to misery. The original Lucius Junius Moderatus Columella was a Roman soldier and tribune of the first century AD, as well as being a farmer and poet

CHAPTER 20 (VOLUME I, CHAPTER XX)

The Palmers

The reader sees the Palmers very much from Elinor's point of view. Mrs Palmer is 'a very silly woman' (p. 97), although perfectly amiable and devoted to the husband who can hardly bring himself to speak to her. Elinor believes that 'his contemptuous treatment of every body' (p. 97) is merely an attempt – which she recognises as commonplace – to appear superior. Mrs Palmer is very anxious for the Dashwood girls to stay with her for the London season, or to visit the Palmers' home at Cleveland, where Mr Palmer is standing as a candidate for election to Parliament, but Elinor and Marianne are determined to avoid doing so.

Mrs Palmer has met Colonel Brandon in London, and has also heard gossip that Willoughby and Marianne are to be married.

> This chapter consists mainly of a comic interlude, with Mrs Palmer playing the role of clown. The authorial viewpoint gives way ever more frequently to that of Elinor, as she firmly takes the central part in the novel.

against the election before the election

frank for me from 1763, it was a privilege of Members of Parliament to have their letters sent by post free of charge. Any letter 'franked' by an MP (i.e. addressed in his own handwriting) was accepted at the parliamentary post office. Mr Palmer shows either his responsibility or his usual grudging nature by refusing in advance to extend this privilege to his wife's correspondence

CHAPTER 21 (VOLUME I, CHAPTER XXi)

More visitors at Barton Park

Hardly have the Palmers returned to their country home before new visitors arrive. Sir John and Mrs Jennings have made the acquaintance in Exeter of Anne and Lucy Steele. Mrs Jennings discovers them to be distantly related and Sir John has promptly invited them to stay. Lady Middleton is dubious about their social standing, but their sycophantic behaviour to her and their apparent devotion to her children soon win her over.

Elinor and Marianne, who are weary of the unrewarding company of their neighbours at Barton Park, reluctantly go to meet the newcomers. The older Miss Steele – Anne – is a plain and garrulous woman nearing thirty; Lucy is pretty and more discreet, but Elinor feels she lacks sincerity and has no wish for a friendship to develop. Sir John, however, is unstinting in his efforts to bring the young women together. One day, when he is gossiping with the Steeles about Elinor's supposed attachment to Edward Ferrars, she is surprised to discover that they already know Edward.

The Steeles are contrasted in this chapter with the two older Dashwood girls, and Jane Austen quickly makes the reader aware that neither Anne nor Lucy is an admirable young woman. Both flatter their hosts to gain favour. Anne is foolish and empty-headed; Lucy is more personable, but lacks candour.

éclat from the French, meaning burst of light; here it refers to personal brilliance
outside of enough tending towards too much

CHAPTER 22 (VOLUME I, CHAPTER XXii)

Elinor receives a terrible blow

Marianne is too direct to be able to tolerate the company of those she does not like, so the Steeles concentrate their interest on Elinor. Her politeness and sense of social duty lead her to spend some time with them, and she finds that Lucy can be entertaining company for a short while, since she is 'naturally clever' and able to be amusing. However, Elinor recognises her serious defects of character, pitying her lack of education but regretting her lack of sincerity and delicacy.

She is astonished one day to be cross-questioned by Lucy about Mrs Ferrars, the mother of Edward and Robert, and dumbfounded when Lucy confides that she has been engaged to Edward for four years. Although shocked, Elinor maintains her self-control, even when Lucy offers proof in the form of a miniature of Edward and a letter in his handwriting, that what she claims is true. It appears that Edward became engaged to her several years earlier, when he was tutored by her uncle, Mr Pratt; he has recently spent a fortnight with her family at Longstaple, Plymouth, and the ring he wears has a lock of Lucy's hair in it.

Elinor's pride and sense of what is appropriate makes it possible for her to maintain her composure until the Steeles have left, but the author leaves the reader in no doubt of the shattering effect that this news has upon her. The reader also becomes aware that Lucy finds a sadistic pleasure in sharing her secret with Elinor, since Sir John has let everyone know something that he is only guessing but which is in fact true – that Elinor is attached to Edward herself.

miniature a very small-scale portrait, usually painted on ivory, and a favourite nineteenth-century keepsake

VOLUME II

CHAPTER 23 (VOLUME II, CHAPTER i)

Elinor thinks things through

In spite of her grief at Lucy's revelation of her longstanding engagement to Edward, upon reflection Elinor remains convinced of Edward's sincere feelings for herself. She guesses that he may well regret his involvement with Lucy and that this may account for his reserve and low spirits on his recent visit. Elinor promised Lucy to keep her secret, so is unable to confide in her mother or sister about the dire news.

She wants to learn more from Lucy, and an opportunity presents itself one evening at Barton Park, when Elinor excuses herself from a game of cards in order to help Lucy finish an elaborate paper basket she is making for Annamaria, Lady Middleton's spoilt daughter. Marianne also avoids playing cards, although with less grace than her tactful sister, and her piano-playing makes a discreet conversation possible.

> Volume II opens with Elinor very much the centre of the reader's sympathy and interest. Her judgement is not destroyed by misery, and she establishes in her own mind a likely explanation for the position in which Edward finds himself. Her strength of character is demonstrated by her ability to cope on her own with deep unhappiness, and her steadfastness contrasts sharply with Marianne's melodramatic reaction to the setback to her romance.

round game a game of cards that does not require partners
to work fillagree to make an article from finely rolled paper spills, in imitation of delicate metal filigree work. Museums often have examples of this popular work of the period, usually known as 'quilling'
Cassino or casino, a card game where eleven points are required to win, the ten of diamonds and the two of spades being known as 'great cass' (two points) and 'little cass' (one point) respectively

CHAPTER 24 (VOLUME II, CHAPTER ii)

Lucy unburdens herself

Under cover of Marianne's playing, and while occupied in helping Lucy with the paper basket she is making, Elinor learns a great deal more about the engagement between Lucy and Edward. Lucy fears the displeasure of Edward's mother, Mrs Ferrars, who she believes will disinherit Edward if she discovers that he is engaged to a penniless girl. Lucy pretends to try to enlist Elinor's help in persuading her half-brother, John Dashwood, to offer a clerical post to Edward, should he take orders in the Church. In spite of her distress and Lucy's provocative remarks, Elinor gives away nothing of her emotions, even when tested by Lucy's asking whether it would be better to give up the engagement, since the possibility of marriage seems remote. She offers no advice, but forms the opinion that Edward is no longer in love with Lucy, and that Lucy has no feelings for Edward, if she ever had, but will not relinquish her hold upon him.

Elinor does her best to avoid further conversation on the subject during the remainder of the Steele sisters' visit to Barton Park – a period of time that extends beyond the Christmas festivities.

Lucy enjoys playing her malicious game with Elinor but, in spite of all the provocation, Elinor maintains her dignity and reveals nothing of her real feelings.

> **Norland living** the post of clergyman for Norland. In Jane Austen's time, many clerical appointments were in the control of people who owned sizeable properties
> **due celebration of that festival** the festival is Christmas, and Jane Austen is making an ironic reference to the material aspects of the celebration which are found to be appropriate by the Middletons

CHAPTER 25 (VOLUME II, CHAPTER iii)

Mrs Jennings's invitation

The London Season is beginning, and Mrs Jennings presses Elinor and Marianne to be her guests in her London house. Knowing how little Marianne likes Mrs Jennings's company, Elinor is surprised to find that her sister is anxious to accept. Realising that an opportunity to see

Willoughby will arise, but hoping herself to avoid meeting Edward, Elinor gives way to pressure from her mother and Marianne and it is agreed that the girls shall go.

Although Elinor herself does not at all wish to go to London with Mrs Jennings, her good nature leads her to accept in her sister's interests.

Portman-square an elegant area of London near Marble Arch

sending Betty by the coach there will not be room in Mrs Jennings's carriage for her personal servant, so she will travel by public coach, which is much less comfortable

poking by myself pottering about on my own

CHAPTER 26 (VOLUME II, CHAPTER iv)

Berkeley Street

The party sets off on the three-day journey to London in the first week of January. On arriving, Marianne loses no time in writing to Willoughby. She expects him hourly, and is shocked to the point of collapse when it is Colonel Brandon rather than Willoughby who calls next day. Feverishly anxious to see Willoughby, who does not appear, Marianne neglects her social duties even more than usual.

Elinor has to apologise for her sister's lack of interest in visitors, and is very worried on her sister's behalf when no contact is made by Willoughby.

direction address

two-penny post the penny post became the two-penny post in 1801. There were up to eight deliveries each day

barouche a four-wheeled horse-drawn carriage for two couples facing each other, the driver at the front

Bond-street an expensive shopping street in London

CHAPTER 27 (VOLUME II, CHAPTER v)

Where is Willoughby?

There is still no sign of Willoughby, and Marianne persuades herself that, because the weather is fine for January, he is shooting or hunting in the country. However, the Dashwoods learn that he is, in fact, in London and must therefore be avoiding a meeting. Elinor writes to her mother about this worrying situation, urging her to find out from Marianne what her formal relationship to Willoughby is. Colonel Brandon is surprised to learn from Elinor that Marianne is not engaged to Willoughby, so far as her family knows; he explains that the supposed engagement is widely spoken of. He reveals his love for Marianne, and Elinor feels deeply sorry for him, but can give him no hope, since she recognises the depth of feeling her sister has for Willoughby.

> Elinor, unhappy in love herself, continues to provide emotional support for Marianne. She feels sympathy, too, for Colonel Brandon, whose worries about her sister's health and unhappiness she shares.

open weather fine weather, without frost
old city friends Mrs Jennings retains friends from her husband's commercial circle, despite the snobbish disapproval of her daughter, Lady Middleton
his card in fashionable circles it was customary to leave an engraved visiting card when the person on whom one was calling was not at home

CHAPTER 28 (VOLUME II, CHAPTER VI)

Willoughby behaves badly

The Dashwoods attend a grand party with Lady Middleton. In the overheated and crowded rooms, Elinor catches sight of Willoughby, who is with a smart young woman. Reluctantly, he comes over to the sisters, obviously embarrassed, and behaves as if he were only slightly acquainted with Marianne. The girls leave early with Lady Middleton, Marianne in a state of semi-collapse. Elinor gets her to bed and reflects upon the wretchedness that lies ahead for poor Marianne.

> Again, Elinor provides firm support for her troubled sister, preventing her from making an exhibition of herself after Willoughby's rejection. In spite of sharing her sister's grief, she is able to make a rational appraisal of the situation.

hartshorn ammonia smelling salts, used to relieve faintness, and originally made from the horns or antlers of deer

CHAPTER 29 (VOLUME II, CHAPTER vii)

An exchange of letters

Marianne is silent next morning, but writes a last letter to Willoughby. His heartless and insulting reply finally puts an end to Marianne's hopes. He returns her letters and her lock of hair, and informs Marianne that he is shortly to be married to another woman. At last, Marianne confides in Elinor: she was never formally engaged to Willoughby but was sure of their feelings for each other. Elinor reads the distressed notes from Marianne which Willoughby has returned and is somewhat shocked at the impropriety of Marianne's behaviour, but her anger with Willoughby knows no bounds. Although she does not say so to her sister, not wishing to upset her further, she cannot help but be glad that Marianne has escaped marriage with such an insolent and dishonest wretch.

Although Elinor asks her to show some pride in her behaviour and not reveal her grief, Marianne is beyond caring about appearances and wants to go home.

> Marianne feels the misery of her situation deeply and gives full vent to her emotions. The reader knows, of course, that Elinor also suffers her own heartbreak but, having promised silence, is unable to unburden herself.

> Elinor, more aware of what the world will think than her headstrong sister, urges Marianne to hold her head high and give no one the satisfaction of seeing her wretchedness.

CHAPTER 30 (VOLUME II, CHAPTER viii)

Willoughby is to marry an heiress

Marianne bears her trouble badly, and Mrs Jennings's well-intentioned kindnesses next day are intolerable to her. Mrs Jennings has learned that Willoughby's extravagant lifestyle has left him in financial difficulties and he is to marry a Miss Grey, who has £50,000 of her own.

Colonel Brandon is one of the guests that evening; he has heard the news from gossip in a stationer's shop he was visiting and, sympathy for Marianne taking precedence over his own hopes, he is not so delighted as Mrs Jennings expects at the departure of a rival in love.

In their different ways, Elinor and Mrs Jennings try to help Marianne through a difficult time. Mrs Jennings means well with her offerings of little treats, but Marianne is too distraught and impatient to show any appreciation – that is left to Elinor.

old fashioned place Colonel Brandon's house has not been subjected to modernisation, and Mrs Jennings – old-fashioned herself – approves of its traditional comforts

stewponds ponds stocked with fish for the table

one shoulder of mutton...drives another down a traditional saying, implying that eating increases appetite; here Mrs Jennings seems to be suggesting that Colonel Brandon will be able to make Marianne forget Willoughby

Constantia wine sweet wine imported from South Africa, one of the little luxuries offered to Marianne by Mrs Jennings

CHAPTER 31 (VOLUME II, CHAPTER ix)

Even worse news of Willoughby

Marianne continues ungrateful to those trying to help her and feels nothing but loathing for Mrs Jennings when she brings a letter to cheer her up: it is not from Willoughby, as she momentarily hopes, but from her mother. Mrs Dashwood knows nothing of recent events and writes of the supposed future of Marianne and Willoughby.

Colonel Brandon calls unexpectedly, intent on speaking to Elinor alone. He has a significant story to tell. Taking up a reference to past history that Elinor remembers, he describes how, when he was a young man, he and his childhood sweetheart, Eliza – who was very like Marianne – were deeply in love. However, against her will, Eliza was married to the Colonel's brother; her unhappiness with this dissolute man ended in divorce after she committed adultery. She was led into a sequence of degrading affairs and when Colonel Brandon returned from his military posting abroad, he found her in a debtors' prison. She was in the last stages of tuberculosis and all he could do was to make her last days comfortable. Since her death, he has looked after her illegitimate daughter, also Eliza. After leaving school, she was put into the care of a sensible woman and the Colonel was pleased with her progress, fully aware that many believed her to be his own daughter.

However, during a visit to Bath with a friend, she disappeared. For eight months the Colonel heard nothing of her until that morning at Barton Hall when he received a letter, forcing him to break the engagement he had for the water party. Eliza Williams had been seduced by Willoughby, who callously left her alone and penniless. The Colonel found her pregnant and about to give birth: she and the baby were now living in the country.

He had met Willoughby only once: they engaged in a duel in which neither was wounded. Elinor agrees with Colonel Brandon that this account of Willoughby's despicable behaviour may well help Marianne to recover from her infatuation.

Following Colonel Brandon's dramatic tale, Willoughby, who entered the novel as a delightful and charming character, is now seen as utterly unreliable and disreputable. It costs Colonel Brandon something to reveal his unhappy past to Elinor, and she is grateful.

exchange Colonel Brandon was able to return home by arrangement with another officer, who took up Brandon's position abroad

spunging-house debtors' prison

consumption tuberculosis, a prevalent and usually fatal wasting disease

met by appointment euphemism for engaging to fight a duel – an illegal activity, except for those in the military, but relatively common none the less

CHAPTER 32 (VOLUME II, CHAPTER X)

Willoughby is married; the Steeles arrive in London

Marianne learns of Willoughby's earlier betrayal, and becomes less passionately grief-stricken, although very melancholy. Elinor manages to prevent the gossipy members of the Middleton party from speaking about Willoughby to Marianne, but she has to suffer endless speculation about him. Shortly afterwards, in February, he is married and leaves London with his bride.

Mrs Dashwood advises the girls to extend their stay in London. Anne and Lucy Steele arrive. Elinor knows that as a result of the extended visit, she will meet Edward, something she had hoped to avoid.

She suffers, too, from Lucy Steele's deliberately provocative conversation on the subject.

> **to have went away** Lucy Steele's grammar is often flawed, as in this example

CHAPTER 33 (VOLUME II, CHAPTER xi)

Enter Robert Ferrars

Marianne goes out of the house for the first time since the final break with Willoughby. Waiting to be served in a jeweller's shop, the sisters are amused to observe a fussy dandy making heavy weather over the purchase of a toothpick case. (He later turns out to be Robert Ferrars, Edward's younger brother.)

They are not sorry to meet their half-brother, John Dashwood, who is also in the shop; he is introduced to Mrs Jennings and calls on them next day. His materialistic approach to life is soon to the fore, however, as he guesses wrongly that Colonel Brandon is interested in marrying Elinor, and asks how much he is worth. He is delighted to meet the Middletons: Lady Middleton has much in common with Fanny.

Elinor is surprised to learn that Mrs Ferrars, Edward's mother, is planning a marriage for him with the Hon. Miss Morton, a wealthy woman.

There is a great deal of comedy in the novel, not least in the ways of some of the characters; John Dashwood, however, is unrelievedly unpleasant. His sisters' mild pleasure at seeing him after several months is soon overtaken by distaste for his selfishness, snobbery and hypocrisy.

> **Exeter Exchange** an indoor zoo, which existed for a time on an upper floor of a merchants' meeting-place near the Strand in central London
> **inclosure of Norland Common** the enclosure of common land was a controversial practice of the period, being to the advantage of landowners, who simply added the land to their own acreage, but to the disadvantage of those who lost the right to graze their animals on the common land

CHAPTER 34 (VOLUME II, CHAPTER xii)

The Dashwoods give a dinner party

Elinor and Marianne are invited to dinner with their brother and Fanny. They are the least important guests, of course: the Middletons and their guests, the Steele sisters, Mrs Jennings and Colonel Brandon are also invited. Elinor is interested to meet the formidable Mrs Ferrars, the mother of Edward and Robert; Lucy Steele, though, is very apprehensive.

Unaware of Edward's involvement with Lucy, Mrs Ferrars and Fanny Dashwood make a great fuss of her, intending to slight Elinor, whom they know to be admired by Edward. Marianne is offended at their treatment of her beloved sister, especially when her painted screens are unappreciated by Mrs Ferrars, so she speaks out rather rashly.

> Elinor understands perfectly well what is happening and is unperturbed by the rudeness of Fanny and Mrs Ferrars. But warmhearted Marianne is unable to remain silent at their treatment of Elinor.

pair of screens fire screens were essential to protect ladies' complexions from being scorched by the roaring fires then common in wealthy homes. Some stood on the floor, but those painted by Elinor were clearly held in the hand

philippic a bitter verbal attack; the term derives from the name given to the fourth-century BC speeches by the Greek orator Demosthenes, who fiercely attacked the corrupt Philip II of Macedon

CHAPTER 35 (VOLUME II, CHAPTER xiii)

A visit from Lucy

Elinor calmly assesses what has happened, and is at least glad that she has no need for further dealings with the snobbish and generally unpleasant Mrs Ferrars. When Lucy Steele calls, Elinor is surprised that she believes she has instantly become a great favourite with Mrs Ferrars and that the path for her and Edward will be smooth.

When Edward calls unexpectedly, Elinor generously and tactfully leaves him alone with Lucy while she goes to fetch Marianne. Marianne's delight at seeing him, and her belief that he and Elinor are committed to each other, cause much embarrassment to Elinor and Edward, and annoyance to Lucy, who is not prepared to leave Edward alone with the Dashwood girls, but stays until he has left.

Lucy's provoking self-satisfaction and spiteful reference to Willoughby's jilting of Marianne bring her even lower in the reader's estimation. Marianne's misunderstanding of the situation and her outspokenness make this a scene of considerable comedy.

CHAPTER 36 (VOLUME II, CHAPTER xiv)

Lucy's optimism increases

Mrs Palmer's baby is born and her mother, Mrs Jennings, wants to be with her daughter, so the Dashwood girls are expected to spend their days with John and Fanny, where the Steele girls are in residence. Fanny does not like Elinor and Marianne, perhaps sensing their superiority, and has invited Anne and Lucy Steele to stay to avoid the necessity of asking her sisters-in-law.

Lucy's hopes remain high, and Elinor sadly comes to the conclusion that she must expect the announcement of an engagement soon.

Elinor meets Robert Ferrars and finds him to be the silly young man she and Marianne had observed earlier at the jeweller's. Their first impression is reinforced by his foolish conversation.

> **Bonomi, Joseph** Italian-born architect (1739–1808), who came to England at the invitation of the highly respected Adam brothers. He later became well-established in his own right

VOLUME III

CHAPTER 37 (VOLUME III, CHAPTER i)

A secret revealed

Mrs Jennings's daughter recovers well after the birth of her baby, so her mother is able to spend more time at home. Elinor and Marianne are relieved that they do not have to see so much of their brother's household.

One day, Mrs Jennings tells them of a great uproar at the John Dashwoods, which has resulted in the ejection of the Steele sisters. Anne, believing her sister to be a real favourite with the family, decides to let Fanny know of the engagement between Edward and Lucy. The reaction of Fanny, John and Mrs Ferrars is predictable: Anne and Lucy are forced to leave immediately and, since Edward insists upon honouring his commitment to Lucy, he leaves his mother's house in the knowledge that his inheritance will go to Robert.

At last, Elinor is able to explain the situation to her sister. Marianne is aghast to think how much Elinor has been suffering herself during the last months, and while patiently supporting Marianne through her own grief.

There is a touching scene between the sisters in this chapter, which goes to the heart of their temperamental differences. Deeply moved at what Elinor must have been suffering, but unable to imagine how she could have continued to present her usual calm and considerate manner to the world, Marianne at first believes that Elinor's feelings for Edward are not really deep. Elinor disabuses her in an untypically passionate speech, and Marianne, perhaps for the first time, recognises that there is nothing unique about her own capacity for suffering. The bond between the sisters is deepened by Marianne's new understanding of her sister's nature.

red-gum a symptom of teething, which – in the case of Mrs Palmer's infant – involves a rash as well as inflamed gums

no conjurer stupid; Mrs Jennings uses words and phrases that were old-fashioned even at the time in which the novel is set

out of place out of work

land-tax a form of taxation on landowners, introduced in the seventeenth century

CHAPTER 38 (VOLUME III, CHAPTER ii)

Two accounts of Lucy's engagement

Walking with Mrs Jennings in Kensington Gardens one unusually fine March Sunday, Elinor meets Anne Steele, who tells her that Edward has

CHAPTER 38 continued

suggested that Lucy should be released from her engagement to him, since he is now without the means to marry. Lucy was not willing to break the engagement, says Anne, who eavesdropped on the private conversation. Edward now hopes to become ordained and find a living as a clergyman.

A different account of the matter is given by Lucy herself in a letter to Elinor. She claims that although she tried to persuade Edward to give her up, he would not hear of it. Elinor knows which version is the truth, but hands over the letter to Mrs Jennings, who is full of sympathy for Lucy, whose true nature she does not suspect.

Shocked that Anne Steele is reporting a private conversation which she has deliberately overheard, Elinor is nevertheless pleased to hear that Edward has made a tactful attempt to end his engagement to Lucy, even though it was unsuccessful.

chimney-board a board placed in front of a large fireplace to hide the empty grate in the warmer months when the fire was not lit

huswifes (from 'housewife') small, handy sewing cases, containing needles, thread and suchlike

My paper reminds me to conclude 'I'm coming to the end of the page': a trite ending to a letter. However, letters were usually confined to one side of the paper, which would be folded and sealed before being sent, as envelopes were not then in use

CHAPTER 39 (VOLUME III, CHAPTER iii)

Colonel Brandon makes an offer

After more than two months of the London season, the Palmers invite Elinor and Marianne to return with them at Easter to their country house in Somerset, from where they will be able to travel home in one day's journey.

Meanwhile, snatches of conversation between a flustered-looking Elinor and Colonel Brandon are overheard by Mrs Jennings. The Colonel is actually asking Elinor to tell Edward that he wants to offer him the modest living connected to his home at Delaford. He little realises the additional pain he is giving to Elinor by asking her to be his emissary, as she at first believes that the living will allow Edward to marry; however, Colonel Brandon makes it clear that he considers the income inadequate for a married man.

Mrs Jennings misinterprets the odd phrases she has overheard and believes that Colonel Brandon has asked Elinor to marry him.

> Unlike Anne Steele, Mrs Jennings does not deliberately try to overhear a private conversation, but curiosity sharpens her hearing, and she is led astray by the few words that reach her.

> Colonel Brandon is a kind person of great social tact and the reader knows he would be horrified to realise that his good intentions might cause pain to Elinor.

200l. per annum £200 per year; such a sum would be a great deal more than a working-class family had to live on, but, according to Colonel Brandon, would be barely sufficient for a single professional man

CHAPTER 40 (VOLUME III, CHAPTER iv)

Mrs Jennings is mistaken

Mrs Jennings and Elinor are at cross-purposes in the conversation that follows Elinor's interview with Colonel Brandon. Mrs Jennings longs to break the news of what she believes to be Elinor's engagement, but Elinor, thinking Mrs Jennings understands what Colonel Brandon's offer actually was, asks her to keep the matter secret until she can speak to Edward. Mrs Jennings interprets this as meaning that Edward is to officiate at the wedding, after his ordination. When Edward coincidentally arrives, she directs him towards Elinor.

When Elinor explains Colonel Brandon's proposition to him, Edward seems unresponsive, but sets off to thank his benefactor, astonished that someone who is not even related to him can show him so much more kindness than his mother and the John Dashwoods. The misunderstanding is then cleared up with Mrs Jennings, who believes that Edward will in fact marry on such an income, and Elinor sadly finds herself believing so, too.

> The comedy of the misunderstanding is balanced by the reader's fear that Elinor will finally lose all hope of Edward's freeing himself from his engagement to Lucy.

CHAPTER 41 (VOLUME III, CHAPTER V)

Robert Ferrars enjoys a joke

Conscientious Elinor feels obliged to call upon Fanny Dashwood, who claims to have been made ill by the discovery of Edward's engagement. She meets her brother, John, as she arrives and he expresses amazement that Colonel Brandon should be so foolish as to offer a living to Edward, when he might have sold it for a good price. It appears that Mrs Ferrars has said that she wishes Edward's engagement had been to Elinor rather than Lucy, as the lesser of two evils, but John Dashwood believes, like Mrs Jennings, that Colonel Brandon is going to marry his sister. John goes to find his wife and Elinor endures an extended and tiresome encounter with Robert Ferrars, who makes fun of his brother and his prospects, and ridicules Lucy's appearance and manners. Fanny Dashwood actually makes an attempt to be agreeable to Elinor.

> Perhaps the reader thinks that Elinor takes her social duties a little too seriously in feeling obliged to call on Fanny, who has behaved so badly to her. It is quite understandable that Mrs Jennings and Marianne will not go. John demonstrates his mercenary and insensitive nature, and Robert Ferrars again appears affected and unpleasant.
>
> **Mrs Dashwood was denied** Mrs Dashwood was not receiving visitors, and therefore said not to be at home
> **his tythes should be raised** Lucy hopes that the tithes (taxes) paid to the church in Edward's parish will be increased, although she seems to think that they will be paid to Colonel Brandon rather than the rector

CHAPTER 42 (VOLUME III, CHAPTER vi)

A visit to Cleveland

Elinor and Marianne leave with Mrs Jennings and her daughter for the Palmers' house in Somerset. While Elinor is happy to go, Marianne, as usual, is in emotional turmoil. On the third day they arrive at Cleveland, soon followed by Mr Palmer and Colonel Brandon.

The visit is more enjoyable than expected for the Dashwood sisters: Elinor finds Mr Palmer a surprisingly courteous and friendly host, and

Colonel Brandon's company is always pleasant. Marianne, pleased to be out of the city, revels in melancholy solitary walks on the Cleveland estate. However, the April weather is treacherous, and she catches a bad cold one damp evening when she imprudently fails to change her wet shoes and stockings.

> Cleveland is a modern house and its grounds are laid out in the taste of the day. Marianne indulges herself in tearful wanderings as she gazes in the direction where Willoughby's house at Combe Magna is situated. Damp weather usually kept genteel women indoors, or to a gravelled or paved area, since their shoes were quite inadequate to cope with wet grass.

Epicurism a taste for refined food and drink. The Greek philosopher Epicurus (341–270 BC) believed in the full sensual enjoyment of life, as he had no expectation of an existence after death

CHAPTER 43 (VOLUME III, CHAPTER vii)

A dangerous illness

Marianne's illness becomes serious and, when the doctor pronounces it infectious, the Palmers feel it necessary to leave for Bath with their new baby. Elinor nurses her sister and is grateful for the unfailing support of Mrs Jennings and Colonel Brandon. Just after the doctor thinks Marianne is over the worst, she suffers a relapse. Her life is feared for, so Colonel Brandon goes to fetch Mrs Dashwood from Barton Cottage.

The crisis passes and Marianne is sleeping peacefully when a deeply relieved Elinor hears horses and carriage wheels. She runs downstairs to meet her mother, only to find that the visitor in the drawing-room is Willoughby.

> This is a dramatic chapter, in which the author builds up tension through Marianne's illness, provides relief by her recovery and then surprises with the sudden reappearance of the scoundrel Willoughby.

> The soundness of Colonel Brandon's character has long been established; Mrs Jennings has appeared sometimes as a tiresome

CHAPTER 43 continued

gossip, but her sterling attributes now come to the fore, and her kindness makes Elinor 'really love her' (p. 261).

a putrid tendency inclining to be infectious

piquet a card game for two

CHAPTER 44 (VOLUME III, CHAPTER viii)

Willoughby explains

Elinor tries to retreat, not wishing to speak to Willoughby and thinking he may be drunk, but he insists on offering an explanation for his conduct. Hearing from Sir John Middleton that Marianne was dying, he has made the journey from London in one day. He had grown to love Marianne at Barton, he says, and intended to ask her to marry him, but his relative, Mrs Smith, learned of his seduction of Eliza Williams and, since he was not prepared to marry her, told him to leave, cutting off all connection with him. He had no knowledge of Eliza's being pregnant and cannot understand why she was unable to contact him. He does not excuse his behaviour in making no further contact with Marianne, nor in writing the cruel letter that ended their relationship, claiming it was dictated by Miss Grey, to whom he had become engaged in the hope of restoring his fortunes.

Appalling though his behaviour has been, the compassionate Elinor can find it in her heart to forgive him, especially as he has lost Marianne, whom he still loves, and is most unhappily married.

The better side of Willoughby is shown here; the reader remembers his charm and open nature from the early chapters of the narration and understands how Elinor is able to forgive him. However, his conduct has been dreadful, not only to Eliza Williams and Marianne, but also in marrying for mercenary reasons a woman whom he cannot love. His grief at his own loss and the pain he has caused Marianne is compounded by the thought that she might marry Colonel Brandon, to whom he has also caused great distress by betraying his ward, Eliza.

porter a thirst-quenching dark malt beer, most often drunk by labourers

over-set to make drunk

noonchine (or nuncheon) a midday snack between breakfast and afternoon dinner

Drury-lane lobby the foyer of the Theatre Royal in Drury Lane

CHAPTER 45 (VOLUME III, CHAPTER ix)

Colonel Brandon confides in Mrs Dashwood

Colonel Brandon and Elinor's mother arrive in a state of great anxiety about what they will find; their relief at Marianne's recovery is in proportion to their fears. During the emotional turbulence of their journey, Colonel Brandon has told Mrs Dashwood of his love for Marianne and his hopes of eventually winning her heart. She is only too happy to do what she can to forward such a marriage, having decided even upon such limited acquaintance that Colonel Brandon is a man of great character. Elinor agrees.

It is typical of Mrs Dashwood, whose daughter Marianne is so like her, that she forms an immediate opinion of Colonel Brandon's good nature. Elinor agrees, of course, that his is a completely trustworthy character, but points out that her view is based not only upon early impressions, but on her experience of his tact and many kindnesses, as well as on what others have to say of him. In this episode, it is Mrs Dashwood's sensibility that is contrasted with Elinor's sense.

CHAPTER 46 (VOLUME III, CHAPTER X)

Home to Barton

Within four days of her mother's arrival, Marianne is able to get up. Colonel Brandon is shocked by the marks of her illness, which remind him of the appearance of his lost love, Eliza, in her final days. Soon, however, Mrs Dashwood and her daughters are able to return home, pleased to make use of Colonel Brandon's carriage, and with Marianne at last recognising the debt she owes to Mrs Jennings's unfailing kindness.

Marianne is still very weak and tearful, but full of gratitude to her sister for all that she has borne on her behalf. Elinor is delighted to see that she has begun to make a return to her former self. She seizes an opportune moment to tell Marianne about Willoughby's visit and attempts an explanation of his conduct, and Marianne is able to listen with a degree of composure.

> Marianne fully recognises all that has been done for her over the preceding weeks, as she gradually starts to return from the self-centredness of love and grief to something like her normal self.

CHAPTER 47 (VOLUME III, CHAPTER xi)

A marriage is reported

Marianne has reached a good degree of self-knowledge, and agrees with her mother and Elinor that she could never have been happy with Willoughby, although she is relieved to have learned from Elinor about his visit when she was thought to be dying, and about his repentance.

Margaret returns from staying with the Careys, and family life resumes something like its normal pattern. Elinor has heard nothing of Edward for some time, and supposes him to be proceeding with his preparation for ordination, when a servant, Thomas, brings unwelcome news. He has seen the newly married Mr and Mrs Ferrars that morning in Exeter, and Thomas has spoken to Lucy, now Mrs Ferrars, in their chaise. Both Mrs Dashwood and Marianne look towards Elinor, whose shock is apparent. Marianne has a fit of hysterics and Elinor has a chance to compose herself, but her mother recognises that Elinor's feelings for Edward have remained constant and reproaches herself for failing to understand her less demanding daughter's needs.

> Jane Austen surprises the reader as well as her heroine with this turn of events. It seems that there is to be no happy ending for poor Elinor.

Nothing could replace him nothing could restore him (to Mrs Dashwood's favour)

CHAPTER 48 (VOLUME III, CHAPTER xii)

Edward calls

Elinor realises that she had always hoped the marriage would not take place, and makes herself wretched imagining Edward's future life with

Lucy at Delaford. She is surprised to have no news from London relatives of the marriage, and looks forward to an account of events from Colonel Brandon. However, the man on horseback who calls is not the Colonel, but Edward himself.

Edward is pale and agitated and has little to say for himself, nervously fidgeting with a scissors-case, which he distractedly cuts to pieces. On a polite enquiry about Lucy's health, he reveals that Lucy is in fact married to his brother Robert – the Mr Ferrars meant by Thomas in his account.

For once, Elinor loses control of her emotions: she rushes from the room and cries her heart out in tears of joy. Edward, recognising Elinor's feelings, falls into silent contemplation and leaves without saying anything further.

> Elinor's admirable composure throughout the vicissitudes of life is not, after all, impenetrable. The reader is perhaps relieved to see her show her feelings for once.

CHAPTER 49 (VOLUME III, CHAPTER xiii)

A proposal of marriage

Edward is free. After a walk in the fresh air, he asks Elinor to marry him and gains Mrs Dashwood's ready approval. He is happier than anyone has ever seen him, reproaches himself for his folly in becoming entangled with Lucy, but is pleased to have been released without dishonour.

Lucy, it appears, has employed her wiles upon Robert, perhaps believing him to be a better catch, but Robert is now banished by his mother. A letter arrives from John Dashwood, recounting the supposed agonies suffered by the family over Robert's runaway marriage, and suggesting that Edward might expect a reconciliation with his mother through Fanny's good offices. Edward is reluctant to make an appeal, but in the end he decides to announce his new engagement and hope for the best.

Colonel Brandon also visits, pleased to see Marianne restored, but rather gloomy about his hopes of ever winning her. Delighted once he learns the truth about Lucy Steele's scheming and Edward's enduring love for Elinor, he leaves with Edward for Delaford to make plans for improvements to the rectory in which Elinor and her husband will eventually live.

There is a good deal of comedy about Edward's visit to propose: his nervous destruction of the scissors-case in the previous chapter, his 'reverie', his walk outside to gain courage and his new-flowering happiness upon acceptance make this resolution of the loyal lovers' situation particularly enjoyable. However, Elinor is not so far lost in the raptures of love to ignore the advantages of a reconciliation with Edward's mother: as always, her sense prevails.

CHAPTER 50 (VOLUME III, CHAPTER xiv)

Marriages

Early in the autumn, Elinor and Edward are married. Edward has been restored to some favour with his mother, although she is not generous. Robert, too, is eventually reconciled with his mother; he was always her unworthy favourite and she soon succumbs to Lucy's flattering ways.

Within two years, Marianne marries Colonel Brandon. She is surprised that her life turns out as it does, but deeply happy with her devoted husband.

Mrs Dashwood and Margaret remain at Barton Cottage, near the Middletons. Elinor and Marianne live very close to one another at Delaford and maintain harmonious relationships between themselves and their husbands. Other characters in the novel live less agreeably: Willoughby's happiness is destroyed through his own fault; Lucy and Robert quarrel, and there is jealousy between Fanny and Lucy and their husbands.

The narrative has an all-embracing **closure**, with all receiving their just deserts – happiness for the virtuous and some sort of wretchedness for the badly behaved or ill-natured.

invent a sweep plan a curved drive (in front of the rectory)

PART THREE

CRITICAL APPROACHES

CHARACTERISATION

A study of the author's characterisation probably offers the most immediate means of beginning a critical approach to the novel as a whole. Jane Austen leaves a fair amount unwritten about her characters, so there is a temptation, which need not necessarily be avoided, for the reader to amplify certain aspects. Physical descriptions are scanty, while a politeness common to most of those who fill her pages sometimes disguises intention: the reader may have to work quite hard to supply some of the more superficial characteristics of Austen's cast. What is essential in making a study of her characters is to examine closely what they say to and about each other, and what the narrator has to say about their thoughts and reactions: this is the crucial evidence on which to base an analysis.

AT BARTON COTTAGE

MRS DASHWOOD

The mother of the two heroines of *Sense and Sensibility* is a woman in her early forties who is widowed at the beginning of the narrative. She is an impulsive and warm-hearted person, who suffers financial disappointment through the greed of her self-serving stepson, and humiliation from his wife. The first she can bear, but the second she finds intolerable: 'in her mind there was a sense of honour so keen, a generosity so romantic' (p. 5) that she is disgusted by the behaviour of Fanny; her impulsiveness is underlined in the first chapter when, but for Elinor's voice of reason, she would have left Norland at once.

She is a cultivated woman, who teaches her youngest daughter Margaret at home – and presumably did the same with Elinor and Marianne. She is whole-hearted – or immoderate – in her affections, saying that she 'can feel no sentiment of approbation inferior to love'

(p. 14).Thus she warms at once to her daughters' admirers – as they do to her. Her 'captivating manners' easily overcome Edward's reserve on his first, gloomy visit to Barton Cottage because, the narrator explains, 'a man could not very well be in love with either of her daughters, without extending the passion to her' (p. 79).

Mrs Dashwood is not a very practical woman: her plans for extending Barton Cottage demonstrate the breadth of her imagination rather than her confidence in the plans' fulfilment. Although her unworldly nature means that she is not always aware of what might be best for her daughters – for instance, her delicacy prevents her from pressing Marianne about the nature of her relationship with Willoughby – she is a fond mother. As the daughters return from London, each with an aching heart, they both look forward to the comfort of her presence, Elinor perhaps less for her own sake than because she knows how much Marianne needs her. By the end of the narrative, Mrs Dashwood has recognised that she has somewhat neglected the self-controlled Elinor for Marianne, the more clamorously emotional daughter who is so much like herself.

The reader is not acutely aware of Mrs Dashwood's shortcomings as a mother because she is absent from the crucial events of the novel that take place in London. However, she often shares the satirical treatment meted out to Marianne's emotional volatility. On the whole, she is sympathetically dealt with by an author who saw nothing sacred about the concept of motherhood, as is demonstrated by her sardonic treatment of Mrs Bennet in *Pride and Prejudice* or Fanny Price's mother in *Mansfield Park*. Austen makes fun of her towards the end of the novel when Mrs Dashwood claims to the unconvinced Elinor, 'There was always a something, – if you remember, – in Willoughby's eyes at times, which I did not like' (p. 287). However, in the novel's tidy **closure**, even Mrs Dashwood demonstrates an unfamiliar prudence; rather than remove to Delaford to be near her older daughters, she stays at Barton Cottage, where Margaret, coming up to a marriageable age, will be able to take advantage of the social life of Barton Place.

ELINOR DASHWOOD

Although the novel can be said to have two heroines, Jane Austen makes it clear that Elinor's is the central role. This is not only because she is at the centre of what happens, but because the **narrative mode** often shifts from **omniscient narrator** to Elinor's viewpoint. Much of the reader's grasp of events in the novel is delivered through both the comments and the thoughts of Elinor.

Her sound character is introduced in Chapter 1: Elinor possesses 'a strength of understanding, and coolness of judgment' (p. 6), but this extreme rationality is softened by adding that the nineteen-year-old 'had an excellent heart; – her disposition was affectionate, and her feelings were strong; but she knew how to govern them' (p. 6). It is not until Chapter 10 that we learn that 'Miss Dashwood had a delicate complexion, regular features, and a remarkably pretty figure' (p. 41) and is taller than her 'still handsomer' sister Marianne. Good looks are never so important for Austen's heroines as qualities of spirit and understanding.

Unlike her sister, Marianne, whose nature is a complete contrast, Elinor values the structure and support offered by society and is prepared to play by its rules. She is discreet and not deceitful, but recognises the social duty of telling white lies when tact and politeness require it. It is her iron self-control that becomes her most striking and perhaps even worrying quality: it is a relief to the reader as well as to herself when she is finally able to reveal the misery she has gone through over Edward's secret engagement to the devious Lucy Steele and, above all, when she breaks down at the end of the novel – although her temporary loss of cóntrol is due to joy rather than grief when she discovers that Edward is free at last. She also, uncharacteristically, has an unprincipled moment, as she allows herself to wish Willoughby's wife dead and he free, when his charm temporarily makes her regret his loss to Marianne and the whole family.

She is a model of conventional behaviour, prepared to attend dinners, balls and parties at Barton Park and in London, even though she does not usually enjoy the company. Even more heroically, she knows when social courtesy requires a visit and calls on the detestable Fanny Crawford, who has treated her so badly, when Fanny claims to be ill.

Elinor often observes these events with a detached and ironic eye, as we learn through the author's use of her central character's viewpoint. She is honourable, keeping Lucy's secret and respecting Edward for his refusal to break his engagement, unhappy though he is, and unhappy though it makes her: Elinor 'gloried in his integrity' (p. 228). She is proud, refusing to let anyone see her own wretchedness, and trying to persuade Marianne to show some self-respect and hide her true feelings after the catastrophic rejection by Willoughby: 'It is a reasonable and laudable pride which resists such malevolence' (p. 160).

The reader may find Elinor's iron grip on her emotions a little daunting, but her powers of reasoning, of working out what is really happening, what really motivates others' actions, are admirable. She is able to examine feelings in a rational light. Her unshaken belief in Edward's love for her is based on her understanding of what has passed between them at Norland; she is able to establish Edward's position in relation to Lucy Steele as clearly as if he had been able to tell her himself. Reason at first causes her to believe that Marianne and Willoughby are engaged when she sees them whispering together and learns that Willoughby has a lock of her sister's hair; but reason, too, causes her to believe that Willoughby does not intend to continue his relationship with her sister, when there is no announcement of an engagement and he fails to communicate with Marianne.

The Dashwoods are a cultivated family, well read and sure of their own taste. Elinor's particular interest is in drawing, a pastime in which the reader finds her occupied on several occasions at Barton. A close and accurate observer of what goes on around her, the practising of detailed figurative drawing seems an appropriate pursuit for her to follow.

MARIANNE DASHWOOD

The seventeen-year-old Marianne is musically talented, with a striking figure and a face, says the narrator, 'so lovely, that when in the common cant of praise she was called a beautiful girl, truth was less violently outraged than usually happens' (p. 41). Throughout most of the narrative, Marianne's characteristics are directly opposed to those of her sister. Fiercely individualistic and impatient of those who do not come up to her high standards in cultural enthusiasm and taste, she is impulsive, indiscreet and imprudent. Passionate in her affections, she does not suffer fools gladly and can be impatient and even rude to those she does not care for. She has an openness and transparency in her dealings with others that may well appeal to present-day readers; contrasted, however, with the discretion and unfailing courtesy of Elinor, such openness can be seen as inappropriate, even dangerous, behaviour for a genteel young woman of that time. When rebuked by Elinor for her indiscretion in driving alone with Willoughby to look over his relative's house, however, she makes a candid claim to an innate sense of virtue: 'if there had been any real impropriety in what I did, I should have been sensible of it at the time, for we always know when we are acting wrong' (p. 60).

Her violent emotions and her exaggerated sensibility (see Part Five, Literary Background) make her appear slightly ridiculous at the beginning of the novel: on leaving Norland, for example, she indulges in a solitary rhetorical farewell to the house and trees, ending with the solipsistic, 'But who will remain to enjoy you?' (p. 23). Her opinions on matters of taste are not to be questioned: she withholds admiration for Edward because he does not have what she considers to be the correct enthusiasms. She believes in the validity only of first love; 'second attachments', as she calls them, can never have her approval.

Falling in love with Willoughby, she behaves not only imprudently, but recklessly, which worries her sister. (Colonel Brandon's later account of the seduction and abandonment of Eliza offers a sombre parallel to the fate that could have resulted from Marianne's unchecked passion.) Her wretchedness when Willoughby leaves suddenly is desperate, but she indulges it, as Elinor observes, for her own melancholy pleasure, and makes no attempt to control her grief. When the rupture is final, she almost dies, making herself ill by walking in wet grass and dreaming about what might have been. She punishes herself, but also those who love her.

Jane Austen makes Marianne a reformed character by the end of the narration: full of new respect for Elinor, who has borne so much in silence, and, of course, contentedly settled in a marriage, which is that 'second attachment' she had previously so much despised. A sense of tragedy averted still lingers around the figure of Marianne, however, and perhaps the reader has an uncomfortable feeling that her free spirit has been crushed in a way that leaves her diminished.

MARGARET DASHWOOD

The reader hears little of thirteen-year-old Margaret, who is peripheral to the action, but useful as an information gatherer about the courtship between Marianne and Willoughby. At the close of the novel, she is moved into the position vacated by Elinor and Marianne, as a pleasing young woman who will help to enliven activities at Barton Park (in much the same way that Austen brings in Fanny's sister, Susan, at the end of *Mansfield Park*). Thus she is a reminder, perhaps – beyond the loose ends that Austen ties up – that, just as some girls are settled satisfactorily in her literary world, there will always be another needing to be found a husband.

AT NORLAND PARK

JOHN AND FANNY DASHWOOD

Although they are the source of much comedy, Mr and Mrs John Dashwood are as black-hearted a couple as any the reader is likely to meet in Jane Austen's novels. Their greed is matched only by their hypocrisy. In Chapter 2, where Austen's mastery of revealing dialogue is evident, John and Fanny are introduced or, rather, uncovered, to the reader. By the end of a private conversation, Mrs Henry Dashwood and her daughters are cheated out of their inheritance, as Fanny persuades her only too amenable husband that he need offer no financial assistance to his stepmother and half-sisters. John begins by proposing to give an ungenerous thousand pounds to each of his sisters, which would be much less than his father intended, but useful none the less. With an ingenious range of arguments, and apparent deference to her spouse, Fanny demolishes her husband's diminishing proposals of assistance in turn, until they are able to agree that their obligations would be more than adequately fulfilled by occasional gifts of fish and game. (Her arguments in sequence are: their small son would be deprived of the money given away; his sisters are only 'half blood' (p. 8) and therefore hardly related; his father was light-headed at the time of the request; an annuity to Mrs Dashwood might tie up money for many years; his father never intended help to include money; his stepmother and sisters will live so modestly that they will in any case have more money than they can spend; Mrs Dashwood will not need a gift of furniture for her house when she moves, since she already has enough.)

Not only are John and Fanny unwilling to part with even a tiny portion of their considerable wealth, but they are completely satisfied with their self-justifications. Fanny is even jealous of what little Mrs Dashwood has in the way of silver plate and good china.

John Dashwood, 'rather cold hearted, and rather selfish' (p. 5), is also rather stupid and his insensitivity and mercenary attitudes – particularly to marriage – are the source of much amusement. Fanny is cleverer, though, and Austen's **irony** does not conceal her real unkindness to Elinor and Marianne, whose superiority she must recognise, although she would never admit it. Good-natured Mrs Jennings does not think much of Fanny on first acquaintance, finding her 'a little proud-looking woman of uncordial address' (p. 194), and she finds Fanny's behaviour outrageous when she unceremoniously ejects the Steele sisters from her house.

MRS FERRARS

Fanny's rich mother is another of Austen's really nasty creations. This minor character is etched in acid by the author: small and sour-looking, 'Her complexion was sallow; and her features small, without beauty, and naturally without expression; but a lucky contraction of the brow had rescued her countenance from the disgrace of insipidity, by giving it the strong characters of pride and ill nature' (p. 196).

With no personal merit, she is important in the narrative because her grasp on the purse strings makes her lack of good will a formidable barrier to Edward's marriage.

EDWARD FERRARS

The most appealing member of the Ferrars family, Edward does not share the unpleasant characteristics of his mother, sister and brother.

During most of the narrative he is in low spirits because of his deeply regretted engagement to Lucy Steele; this makes it impossible for him to speak to Elinor of his love for her, although she is sure of it. Consequently, he appears to be a rather dull young man – as Marianne complains to her mother. Admitting that Edward is 'amiable' enough, she says, 'there is something wanting – his figure is not striking; it has none of that grace which I should expect in the man who could seriously attach my sister. His eyes want all that spirit, that fire, which at once announce virtue and intelligence' (pp. 14–15). Worse, he has no taste and reads aloud without enough emotion to suit the passionate Marianne. Later, Eleanor counters with a view based upon her more intimate knowledge of Edward: she praises his obvious 'sense and goodness' and adds, 'I venture to pronounce that his mind is well-informed, his enjoyment of books exceedingly great, his imagination lively, his observation just and correct, and his taste delicate and pure' (p. 17). She adds that although he is not handsome at first sight, 'the general sweetness of his countenance' makes up for that.

Even without Elinor's testimony, the reader is made aware that Edward is not without engaging characteristics. Pretending to know nothing of the aesthetic theory relating to the **picturesque**, he teases Marianne about the ways to appreciate a Devonshire landscape, showing a gentle sense of humour and that he is actually perfectly at home with the subject (pp. 84–5).

Always rather shy, and suffering from the delightful shock of learning that Lucy has freed him, he presents himself at Barton Cottage in order to propose to Elinor. Unable to find the words to explain his presence to the assembled company, he absent-mindedly picks up some scissors and snips their case to pieces – offering a visual image that brings him very much to life.

Lonely and lost for most of the narrative, into which he enters only occasionally, by the end he is a twenty-four-year-old firmly anchored in life: married to the loyal Elinor and having found a vocation in the Church (see Part Five, Social Background).

ROBERT FERRARS

The younger brother of Edward, and a very minor character, Robert is a vain and foolish would-be dandy. Elinor feels a 'contempt' (p. 252) for him that anyone less self-centred would notice. He serves a useful purpose in the plot, since the scheming Lucy transfers her attention to him as a potentially wealthier prospect than his brother. His mother's favourite, he is soon forgiven by her and retains the inheritance she transferred to him on learning of Edward's engagement to Lucy.

AT BARTON PARK

SIR JOHN MIDDLETON

From the moment he offers an affordable home to his cousin, Mrs Dashwood, Sir John is clearly established as very different from her nearer relative, John Dashwood. Generous and hospitable, he makes his cousin and her daughters very welcome at Barton and cannot do enough for them. However, his cordiality and constant desire for company conceal a shallowness and fear of being alone. He enjoys the country sports offered by his estate and entertains lavishly at Barton Park. He enjoys the company of young people in particular, and, we learn, 'was a blessing to all the juvenile part of the neighbourhood, for in summer he was forever forming parties to eat cold ham and chicken out of doors, and in winter his private balls were numerous enough for any young lady who was not suffering under the insatiable appetite of fifteen' (p. 28).

However, the cultivated Dashwoods find social events at the big house usually tedious and the company of Sir John and his wife unrewarding. He is insensitive and enjoys teasing young women, in a heavy-handed way, about their supposed romantic prospects. Elinor, recognising his underlying good nature and her social duty, is always civil, but Marianne is outspoken and even rude when he uses a phrase she finds particularly offensive, joking that she might be 'setting her cap' at a young man (p. 40).

Although Sir John is not nearly perceptive enough to understand the intricacies of the narrative's various love affairs, he plays a pivotal role in that virtually all the characters meet at Barton Park and/or at the Middletons' London house.

LADY MIDDLETON

The dull daughter of Mrs Jennings is a surprising wife for Sir John, and perhaps the reason for his constant need of additional company. Her elegant houses are perfectly run, and she offers a lavish table to suit Sir John, but she has little interest beyond her four spoilt children and domestic matters. Worse, she has a chilly personality and is described damningly as having a 'cold insipidity' that is 'repulsive' (p. 30). Unsurprisingly, Lady Middleton and Fanny Dashwood appear to be soul mates: when they meet, we learn that 'There was a kind of cold hearted selfishness on both sides, which mutually attracted them; and they sympathized with each other in an insipid propriety of demeanour, and a general want of understanding' (p. 194).

MRS JENNINGS

Introduced as 'a good humoured, merry, fat, elderly woman, who talked a great deal, seemed very happy, and rather vulgar' (p. 29), Mrs Jennings is, surprisingly, Lady Middleton's mother. She has a great deal more in common with Sir John than with her daughter and, in the first part of the novel, the Dashwoods find her company unwelcome; Marianne avoids her and Elinor suffers from this 'everlasting talker' who takes a great fancy to her.

It is only Marianne's desire to be near the departed Willoughby that causes the Dashwood girls to accept Mrs Jennings's invitation to her London house for the winter season. But, as the narrative unfolds, Mrs Jennings's gossipy, inquisitive and coarse characteristics are outweighed by her great kindness, her 'active good nature' (p. 290) and sincerity. In spite of her snobbish daughter's distaste, Mrs Jennings is not prepared to give up her old friends 'in trade', and her judgements about the behaviour of Fanny Dashwood and Mrs Ferrars are sound. Her real worth is shown during Marianne's illness, when her help and support are invaluable. By the end of the novel, Elinor is able to feel that she 'really loves' Mrs Jennings (p. 261), and a more sober Marianne recognises what she owes her.

Among the secondary players in the narrative, Mrs Jennings is notable for the way in which her character blossoms. Something of a figure of fun at the beginning, her genuine warmth has given her a broader dimension by the end of the novel.

MR AND MRS PALMER

This apparently ill-matched pair make brief appearances at Barton Park, at their London house and finally at their country house, Cleveland. Mr Palmer is proud, silent and disdainful of his silly wife, while she is always laughing and pretending amusement at his scornful treatment of her. Charlotte Palmer is Mrs Jennings's younger, much-loved daughter, and the birth of her first child preoccupies Mrs Jennings for some time in London, helping the plot forward as the Dashwoods have to spend some time at the Middletons' house. The plot also requires somewhere isolated for Marianne to be ill, and Cleveland serves this purpose, as the girls stay there on their long journey home to Barton Cottage.

ANNE AND LUCY STEELE

Like the Dashwood sisters, the Steeles are young women with very little money, but there the similarity ends. They are invited to Barton Park on the strength of their distant relationship to Mrs Jennings and are strongly contrasted with Elinor and Marianne.

Anne, the elder sister, 'nearly thirty, with a very plain and not a sensible face' (p. 102), is a clownish figure in the narrative. Unmarried, she clings, apparently without justification, to the notion that a Dr Davies in her home town, Exeter, is attracted to her, and chatters incessantly about beaux. Garrulous and tactless, she is an embarrassment to her sister, Lucy, who leaves Anne stranded at the end of the narrative, having borrowed all her money, then left her behind to run away with Robert Ferrars.

Lucy is an attractive girl in her early twenties: 'her features were pretty', the Dashwoods acknowledged, 'and she had a sharp quick eye, and a smartness of air, which, though it did not give actual elegance or grace, gave distinction to her person' (p. 102). Lucy is Elinor's rival, having become engaged to Edward four years earlier when he fell in love with her, and unwilling to release him now that he has changed his mind. She is shrewd and spiteful, enjoying the torment she causes Elinor with her detailed – and self-flatteringly edited – accounts of her relationship with Elinor's beloved Edward. She has an eye on her financial advantage, and turns out to be a manipulative and successful social climber, when she seizes her chance to ensnare Robert Ferrars. She is even able to worm her way into the affections of the dreadful Mrs Ferrars after she has run away with her favourite son. The last glimpse of Lucy, however, is not a happy one. Jane Austen gives an ironic account of her fate: 'setting aside the jealousies and ill-will continually subsisting between Fanny and Lucy, in which their husbands of course took a part, as well as the frequent domestic disagreements between Robert and Lucy themselves, nothing could exceed the harmony in which they all lived together' (p. 320).

COLONEL BRANDON

A retired army friend of Sir John's and frequently at his house, although his quiet and considerate nature is very different from that of his boisterous host. Much too old for marriage at thirty-five, in the eyes of Marianne, the Colonel's devotion to her nevertheless increases throughout the narrative. He is finally successful in winning her affections after she eventually recovers from her disastrous love affair with the rakish Willoughby.

Marianne sees the Colonel as an ancient and decrepit arthritic when she first meets him, on the basis of his liking a flannel waistcoat in cold weather. It is a long time before she recognises his true worth – unlike Elinor, whose rapport with him is so sympathetic that they are thought to be in love by some of their acquaintances. Although, like most of Austen's men, he is not a strong presence in the narrative, the reader warms to his sensitivity and reliability.

In fact, Colonel Brandon is much nearer to being a **romantic** hero that Marianne could admire than might be supposed. His melancholy is the result of an unhappy love affair as a young man, and one which has taken some melodramatic turns. His lost love fell into a social outcast's life of scandalous relationships, and on her death he became the guardian of her illegitimate daughter. He finds much that reminds him of his lost love in Marianne's looks and temperament. These events, together with the duel he fights with his ward's seducer, Willoughby, could certainly form part of the life story of a man of sensibility, and perhaps Marianne's eventual marriage to him is not quite the second best that it is often said to be.

JOHN WILLOUGHBY

One of Jane Austen's most successful rakish characters, Willoughby's allure is evident, especially in this novel where the competition consists of the quiet and pensive Colonel Brandon and the despondent Edward Ferrars. He makes his initial appearance performing the romantic task of rescuing a maiden in distress, and his impact upon those at Barton Cottage is immediate: he spoke 'in a manner so frank and so graceful, that his person, which was uncommonly handsome, received additional charms from his voice and expression' (p. 38). Sir John speaks up for him in terms the reader would expect, as being 'As good a kind of fellow as ever lived, I assure you. A very decent shot, and there is not a bolder rider in England' (p. 39).

He is made welcome at Barton Cottage by Marianne's grateful family and joins in their activities. Unlike Edward Ferrars, he is apparently an excellent reader: *Hamlet* remains unfinished when he leaves. (To be a good dramatic reader is not necessarily a recommendation in Austen's male characters, however: the attractive but immoral and ultimately unworthy Henry Crawford in *Mansfield Park* is able to move his hearers almost to tears.)

Marianne decides that Willoughby is everything she looks for in a lover, and they enjoy idyllic days which everyone expects to lead to marriage. But, alas for Marianne, he has loved and left at least one other girl, and callously abandons Marianne when his extravagance leaves him in financial difficulties and prompts him to marry a wealthy heiress instead. He makes no attempt to soften the cruelty of his breach with Marianne, and his casual abandonment of the pregnant Eliza Williams reveals that his charm conceals a selfish and dishonourable nature.

Even Elinor, a better judge of character than the rest of her family, succumbs to that charm when Willoughby arrives seeking forgiveness during what he believes to be Marianne's fatal illness. She even feels sorry for him, though she recognises the power of his charisma: she thinks of

CHARACTERISATION continued

his loss to her family 'with a tenderness, a regret, rather in proportion, as she soon acknowledged within herself – to his wishes than to his merits. She felt that his influence over her mind was heightened by circumstances which ought not in reason to have weight; – by that person of uncommon attraction, that open, affectionate, and lively manner which it was no merit to possess; and by that still ardent love for Marianne, which it was not even innocent to indulge' (p. 283).

THEMES

Sense and Sensibility has a big main theme announced by the title. Overtly, the narrative sets out to persuade the reader that common sense is crucial to meet life's challenges and that this precludes indulgence in an exaggerated **sensibility**. The plot supports this theme, in that the ending rewards sense, in the person of Elinor, who marries the man she loves, and punishes Marianne, who loses her love and almost dies, although she is allowed a somewhat unconvincing happy ending. While the plot supports this moral lesson, the novel is an ambivalent one, and much of what follows in this Note relates to the different reading that emerges as the darker side of this comedy becomes apparent (see Part Six, Critical History). This different reading acknowledges the merit of some of Marianne's emotional understanding and finds Elinor's reserve and rigid self-control verging upon the destructive.

Secondary themes, familiar to readers of other novels by Jane Austen, relate to honour, loyalty and their opposites; to money and marriage; to the growth of maturity in young women; and to the hollowness of social pretensions.

Much of what is so discreetly said in *Sense and Sensibility* was more candidly treated in the young Austen's short epistolary novel, *Love and Friendship*. In that she creates high comedy when dealing with the ostentatious sensibilities of her characters. In fact, her juvenilia was marked by a riotous imagination and a ready acknowledgement of the existence of sexual misdemeanours.

Houses are important in Jane Austen's work, and often achieve ambivalent symbolic status: the grand house that gives the title to *Mansfield Park*, for instance, stands for order and luxury for Fanny Price, the heroine of that novel, in contrast to her own slovenly home, yet its owners produce decadent children; the reality of Northanger Abbey, comfortably modernised, mocks the romantic expectations of its heroine, Catherine Morland, fed upon Gothic novels and anticipating intriguing ruins. (As those who have read it will know, the sense versus sensibility argument is given a more light-hearted airing in *Northanger Abbey*.) In *Sense and Sensibility* the narrative unfolds in four country houses and in their owners' London establishments.

Norland Park is an old and apparently handsome property set in well-established grounds, at first the beloved home of Mrs Henry Dashwood and her girls, but soured for them by its passing to the selfish and greedy John and Fanny Dashwood. The house's stability as a home is undermined for those who live in it by the vagaries of inheritance laws (a situation paralleled for the Bennets in *Pride and Prejudice*). John Dashwood's account of the expensive so-called 'improvements' to his property is heard with dismay by Elinor – a dismay that the reader is expected to share. 'The old walnut trees' have been pulled down to accommodate an imposing greenhouse, which, John says, 'will be a very fine object from many parts of the park' (p. 191). This insensitive type of modernisation is mocked elsewhere in Austen's works, particularly in *Mansfield Park*, where a fine avenue of ancient trees is to be pulled down at Sotherton to make way for 'improvements'.

Norland thus comes to represent the displacement of traditional values by damaging modernisation applied by people with more money than taste.

Barton Cottage, at first just a refuge for Mrs Dashwood and her daughters, soon becomes a happy home. The narrator explains, with humorous **irony**, 'as a cottage it was defective' because it is, in fact, a new, modern house, lacking the traditional accessories of thatch and romantic climbing plants. However, this relatively humble stone-built house, set in beautiful countryside, represents peace and contentment, as the Dashwoods employ themselves about their artistic and intellectual interests. The modest but genuine hospitality offered by Mrs Dashwood contrasts with the hectic social life at Barton Park, and visitors appreciate it. Although the fact that it is Marianne's home makes it especially precious to Willoughby in the early days of his happiness with her, his exclamation, 'Improve this dear cottage! No.' (p. 63) suggests that the ways in which the Dashwoods have made their house welcoming are very appealing. There is an unusually detailed account of the house (p. 24), with its two sitting rooms, four bedrooms and two attic rooms (for the servants), and at the back 'dark narrow stairs, and a kitchen that smokes' (p. 64).

Mrs Dashwood dreams of improvements of a practical kind, although the reader knows that her limited means rule out such a plan. Barton Cottage has a fully realised presence in the novel, partly because of its supposed limitations perhaps, and this certainly helps to convey the well-established view that happiness does not depend upon wealth and luxury.

Barton Park seems to be the social hub of the area. The house is 'large and handsome' and the Middletons live there 'in a stile of equal hospitality and elegance' (p. 28). The lives of Sir John and Lady Middleton are empty, except for his sporting interests and her devotion to the children; the constant stream of visitors and guests disguises the shallowness of their lives, Sir John enjoying the company and Lady Middleton the opportunity to display the refinement of her domestic arrangements. In spite of Barton Park's elegance and comforts, the Dashwood girls find most of the company tedious and the conversation usually dull; Marianne tries to avoid social visits. Nevertheless, the scene of so much busy socialising offers the opportunity to forward the events of the first part of the novel, and there is perhaps a wry acknowledgement that young women can come by acceptable husbands through participation in the kind of social opportunities provided by Sir John. The chastened Marianne eventually accepts a husband – wealthy and of good character, if rather old – whom she has met in Sir John's drawing-room. The last page of the novel suggests that Margaret will also find a husband there.

The 'sense' of Elinor recognises that everyone has a part to play in society, and she acknowledges this by fulfilling her social duties, at Barton Park and elsewhere, even if this is sometimes against her inclinations. Marianne, who meets her first love outdoors rather than at Sir John's house, is unwilling to fall in with society's expectations;

she values sincerity, which she feels is sometimes undermined by convention.

Cleveland, the country house of the Palmers, is another comfortable and commodious place; the grounds, described in considerable detail on pages 256–7, appeal very much to Marianne's sensibility. So far as the plot is concerned, it is a conveniently distant place for her to fall sick, away from London and Barton. It also offers the last occasion on which she indulges her exaggerated emotions. The grounds are described by Jane Austen as 'like every other place of the same degree of importance', that is to say, satisfying the contemporary taste for the 'pleasure-grounds' of a large country house. What appeals especially to Marianne is the hilltop Grecian temple, typical of the follies (decorative architectural features with no practical purpose) admired for their **picturesque** qualities. From this vantage point, Marianne gazes yearningly towards the horizon in the direction of Willoughby's house. Her walks in the remoter parts of the grounds, 'where there was something more of wildness than in the rest, where the trees were the oldest, and the grass was the longest and wettest' (p. 259), complement her grief-stricken state and bring her near to a death (which she perhaps desires) after she catches a chill there.

London, like Bath, can have a dubious moral tone in Austen's works, and certainly her heroines are more at home in the country villages and estates that are their natural habitat. In *Sense and Sensibility*, London is the scene of Marianne's final betrayal by Willoughby, as he gives her up to marry an heiress. His loveless but profitable marriage is perfectly understood by London society, even though members of the Middletons' circle are shocked.

It was the practice of wealthier gentry to spend the winter season in London, going to theatres and concerts, and entertaining with balls and parties, which offered good matchmaking opportunities for the parents of the young. The Dashwood girls and the Steeles, without money, are there as a result of invitations from prosperous relatives, who either own London houses, or rent them for the season.

Elinor and Marianne, both unhappy in love, find little pleasure in the somewhat feverish social scene, the discomforts of which are typified by the description of the party at which Willoughby snubs Marianne. They go into 'a room splendidly lit up, quite full of company, and insufferably hot' and endure the miseries of 'saying little and doing less' as they 'take their share of the heat and inconvenience, to which their arrival must necessarily add' (p. 148).

However, the London setting provides an opportunity for Austen to bring together most of her characters and to advance the plot.

NARRATIVE MODES

An **omniscient narrator** is in charge of *Sense and Sensibility*, that is, a narrator who is able to describe the thoughts as well as the actions of the characters and who knows more than any one of them. The narrator is generally concerned with forwarding the events that make up the story, but occasionally offers some direct commentary to the reader: see, for instance, p. 13 where 'the growing attachment' between Elinor and Edmund is alluded to in the narrator's **ironic** view of the general motives of mothers with unmarried daughters.

> Some mothers might have encouraged the intimacy from motives of interest, for Edward Ferrars was the eldest son of a man who had died very rich; and some might have repressed it from motives of prudence, for, except a trifling sum, the whole of his fortune depended on the will of his mother. But Mrs Dashwood was alike uninfluenced by either consideration...'

Among the other occasions when the narrator is in evidence is p. 208, when Austen writes, 'I come now to the relation of a misfortune...' The narrator's relationship with the reader is an easy one, inviting enjoyment of the tale to be unfolded, but also making assumptions about the reader's complicity with the **tone**.

Should we identify the narrator with Jane Austen herself? Critics of narrative style argue over this point, and it certainly cannot be taken as a general rule that author and narrator are one. Many readers, however, like to believe that, particularly at the opening and closing of her novels, the author's own **voice** is present; others believe that the narrator is, as it were, another character in a novel's structure.

The omniscient narrative voice, however, is not always present. Much of *Sense and Sensibility* consists of the thoughts of the characters and, of course, dialogue or conversation, which excludes the presence of the narrator. Chapter 3 clearly shows the revelation of character, not only by the narrator's description, but most effectively by what John and Fanny Dashwood say to each other in their despicable cheating of their step relations. There is an ongoing debate between Elinor and Marianne throughout the novel about sense and sensibility, which is not only implied by their behaviour as described by the narrator, but also made evident in their conversations. In the following extract, for example, after a humorous but quite cruel analysis of Marianne's character, Elinor explains to Edward how she is often aware of making the wrong judgements about others' natures, and Marianne takes the opportunity to snipe at her sister about what she sees as weak-spirited conformity. Elinor, of course, soon puts her right:

> 'I have frequently detected myself in such kind of mistakes,' said Elinor, 'in a total misapprehension of character in some point or other: fancying people so much more gay or grave, or ingenious or stupid than they really are, and I can hardly tell why, or in what the deception originated. Sometimes one is guided by what they say of themselves, and very frequently by what other people say of them, without giving oneself time to deliberate and judge.'
>
> 'But I thought it was right, Elinor,' said Marianne, 'to be guided wholly by the opinion of other people. I thought our judgments were given us merely to be subservient to those of our neighbours. This has always been your doctrine, I am sure.'
>
> 'No, Marianne, never. My doctrine has never aimed at the subjection of the understanding. All I have ever attempted to influence has been the behaviour. You must not confound my meaning. I am guilty, I confess, of having often wished you to treat our acquaintance in general with greater attention; but when have I advised you to adopt their sentiments or conform to their judgments in serious matters?'
>
> (p. 82)

Jane Austen was one of the first English novelists to use a narrative device usually known as **free indirect speech** or **discourse**, which fuses the voices of narrator and character, as when Elinor is anxiously awaiting the return of Colonel Brandon, who is bringing her mother to Marianne's sickbed:

> The time was now drawing on, when Colonel Brandon might be expected back. At ten o'clock, she trusted, or at least not much later, her mother would be relieved

> from the dreadful suspense in which she must now be travelling towards them.
> The Colonel too! – perhaps scarcely less an object of pity! – Oh! – how slow was
> the progress of time which yet kept them in ignorance! (p. 267)

The switch from the voice of the narrator to that of Elinor is hardly
perceptible, even though it is indicated here by the flurry of dashes and
exclamation marks, pointing to her highly charged emotions. It is
Austen's purpose to keep Elinor at the centre of her novel and she does
this in the ways already indicated, as well as by offering an account of
events frequently seen from the heroine's viewpoint, whenever Elinor is
present at a social gathering or taking part in an intimate scene. The
reader will notice, too, that the narrator's **voice** and Elinor's voice bear
many similarities; Elinor's balanced statements and well-chosen phrasing
can echo the narrator's style, and this gives further strength to her
position as the novel's central figure.

TIME

Although no early drafts exist, it is generally accepted that Jane Austen
had completed the first version of *Sense and Sensibility* as early as 1795.
Her sister, Cassandra, remembered the family hearing it read to them
before 1796, and at that stage it was an **epistolary novel** called *Elinor and
Marianne* (see Part Five, Literary Background, for Austen's influences).
It was rewritten under its familiar title in 1797–8 and revised again in
1809–10, before publication in 1811.

Discussion about the nature of **sensibility** was at its height at the
end of the eighteenth century, as was the theory of the **picturesque**, so by
the date of publication, these subjects were not quite so topical. Austen,
however, intended her work to be read as a novel set at the time of
publication, so she made a few minor revisions to bring it up to date.
These included references to the postal service and to popular writers of
the day. For her first readers, therefore, the main events of the novel
could be taken as more or less contemporaneous.

Jane Austen applies a tight time-scheme to her novels, the central
events usually taking place over six to twelve months. In *Sense and
Sensibility*, six months elapse between the death of Henry Dashwood's
uncle and the departure of Mrs Dashwood and her daughters for

Devonshire. They arrive at Barton Cottage in the autumn of one year and Edward Ferrars proposes to Elinor in late spring of the following year, so the main events of the narrative occur within eight or nine months. The marriage takes place in the early autumn and the narrator then looks forward to describe the future contentment or otherwise of the novel's main characters.

During the main time-span of autumn to late spring, events take place in a chronologically straightforward way. In an essay on aspects of Jane Austen's work, David Lodge writes about the reader's experience of time in different genres of fiction: the tempo of a thriller, for instance, can seem faster than reality, while that of a **stream of consciousness** novel might seem slower. But Jane Austen's novels, he writes, 'seem to have the tempo of life itself, yet their stories occupy several months, and the reading of them takes only a few hours' (*After Bakhtin*, 1990, p. 125). Lodge attributes Austen's success in creating something that seems like 'real' time largely to her presentation of events in a series of scenes in which conversation dominates. He describes conversation as 'neutral' in narrative time, since it takes about the same time as hearing it would.

There are no major chronological dislocations in the narrative, although many of the characters are stranded elsewhere in parallel time at some points in the novel. Travelling times, too, were extended, so that there is a sense that when the sisters were at Cleveland, for instance, their mother was cut off not only by distance but by time. Chronological steadiness is maintained, however, by the constant presence in the novel of Elinor and Marianne at Barton Cottage, London and Cleveland.

STRUCTURE

Both the narrative modes and the time pattern help to establish the structure of a novel. The demands of the plot and the realisation of themes are also key elements. In the case of *Sense and Sensibility,* the plot structure follows that required by the **sentimental novel** (see Part Five, Literary Background), of which Samuel Richardson's *Pamela: or Virtue Rewarded* (1740) is a classic example, and one admired by Jane Austen. This **genre** requires a happy ending in which the heroine marries the man she loves after a series of difficulties has been overcome. Elinor and

Edward fulfil this pattern, Elinor having to endure the misery of seeing her beloved unhappily engaged to another woman, an entanglement from which he is freed only after his sudden change of fortune makes Lucy throw him over for his brother. It is the obstacles in the way of the heroine's happiness that create the tension in the structure.

In the case of *Sense and Sensibility*, of course, there is a second heroine to be considered. Although her situation shadows her sister's to some extent, and doubles, as it were, the effect, its resolution is different. Marianne's first love betrays her and she has to accept another man, who has always loved her, but whom she has to learn to love. In Marianne's case, the author gives precedence to demonstrating the superiority of sense over sensibility, not altogether fulfilling the predictable demands of the sentimental novel. Both sisters enjoy a traditional 'happy ending', but there is a sense in which Marianne's spirit has been broken in order to bring her to conformity, and this adds a touch of darkness – even tragedy – to the tale.

LANGUAGE AND STYLE

The long tradition of narrative **realism** was in its early stages at the time Jane Austen was writing, but she developed it to a high degree within the constraints she set herself. The main factor limiting her scope is her preference for the familiar. She wrote to her niece, Anna Austen, who wanted to become a novelist, '3 or 4 families in a Country Village is the very thing to work on' (1814). Writing in 1816 to her nephew, James-Edward Austen-Leigh, she described her famous view of her own work: 'the little bit (two Inches wide) of Ivory, on which I work with so fine a brush, as produces little effect after much labour'. In spite of this clear account of her set purpose, as a kind of domestic miniaturist, she has often been attacked for ignoring the bigger picture – wars, politics, social problems and sex, for instance (see Part Six, Critical History, for further comment on these supposed shortcomings).

That Austen is so widely read nearly 200 years after her novels first appeared is indicative, however, of the value of her work, and perhaps what is always admired is the wit and elegance of her narratives. The harmony of style in her work by no means limits its variety, and the defining elements of Austen's style can be said to be the range of narrative techniques described earlier. The **authorial voice**, or the **omniscient narrator**'s voice, demands a formal and almost judicial style, which can be censorious in relation to characters' shortcomings, but is usually well leavened with humour and **irony** (see Text 3 analysis, pp. 81–5, about this aspect of Austen's work).

Free indirect speech, of which there is less than usual in *Sense and Sensibility*, and narrative with a character-based viewpoint – most frequently that of Elinor – show a marked shift in style to a' lighter tone; this usually has the effect of increasing the pace of the narrative. **Direct speech**, of which there is a great deal in the form of various conversations, offers the opportunity of character development – strikingly in Chapter 3, where the greed and self-satisfaction of John and Fanny Dashwood is revealed, and more gradually elsewhere. All Austen's characters tend to be defined by their conversation at least as much as by description and action, and this requires appropriate speech patterns. The Dashwoods express themselves elegantly, even when moved (see analysis of Texts 1 and 2, pp. 74–81). Sir John, however, has the country squire's bluntness and limited vocabulary, as for example when he is teasing Marianne about her interest in Willoughby: 'Aye, aye, I see how it will be,' said Sir John, 'I see how it will be. You will be setting your cap at him now, and never think of poor Brandon.' Marianne, offended, describes the hackneyed phrase he has used as 'gross' (p. 40).

Mrs Jennings's conversation is gossipy, sometimes even indelicate, and her language is rather vulgar. She occasionally uses old-fashioned colloquial expressions, as when she states that Colonel Brandon's ward is 'as like him as she can stare' (p. 59), or refers to 'poking by myself' (p. 130), meaning pottering about on her own. Mrs Jennings is the garrulous and cheerful widow of a wealthy tradesman and makes few pretences to refinement. The Steele sisters, however, are anxious to promote their claim to gentility, but this is undermined by the grammatical mistakes they sometimes make (see Text 1 analysis, pp. 74–8).

Some letters are exchanged at crucial moments in the narrative; these, like direct speech, offer character development. Marianne's pitiful letters to Willoughby show her frank and direct nature. His to her, which he subsequently claims was dictated by his wealthy bride-to-be, displays nothing but insensitivity and insulting arrogance. Lucy Steele's letters are full of sly hints about Edward which are intended to wound Elinor; her use of well-worn phrases and her uncertain grasp of the finer points of grammar underline what is already known of her. Her final letter, breaking off her engagement, is received with relief by Edward, but he tells Elinor that he has 'blushed over the pages of her writing' and refers to 'the defects of her stile' (p. 310).

Jane Austen's use of **direct speech** is generally deployed in a series of greater or lesser 'scenes' – an appropriate term, since they contain much dialogue, as in a play. She assembles her characters – two, three or more – usually indoors, in a sitting room, or a drawing-room, at a dining table, or at an evening party. Thus, the events of the novel are more often than not conveyed to the reader via what is said on these occasions.

The constraints of indoor meetings do not apply outdoors, it seems (except for a walk in crowded Kensington Gardens, where the ambience is almost that of the drawing-room). Outdoors can be dangerous territory in Austen's novels: for instance, Louisa Musgrove in *Persuasion* badly injures her ankle when jumping off the Cobb at Lyme Regis, and wanderings in the grounds at Sotherton in *Mansfield Park* leave the young people's love affairs in a tangled state. Marianne's troubles originate on a country walk. The events that happen outside are either off stage or without conversation: Marianne's twisted ankle and rescue by Willoughby are described by the narrator without dialogue; Marianne's imprudent trip in Willoughby's barouche to his relative's house and grounds is reported – when found out – by Marianne; similarly, her nearly fatal wanderings in the rain are solitary and therefore without dialogue.

Given Austen's self-imposed constraints of writing from experience or observation, it is not surprising that there are no scenes in which only men are present, except for those that are reported, such as the encounter between Colonel Brandon and Willoughby after the latter's seduction of Brandon's ward has been discovered.

There is not a great deal of what might be called descriptive writing in *Sense and Sensibility*. A plan of Barton Cottage is offered, but other houses are described merely as 'old' or 'modern-built'. Cleveland's gardens are thoroughly described, and the Devonshire countryside gets rather more than a passing reference, particularly during a discussion relating to the **picturesque**. Although the appearance of Elinor and

Marianne is indicated more fully than usual (p. 41), generally characters might be dark or fair, handsome or plain, while a dress might be becoming or otherwise – little else is offered. The reader has a good deal to do in supplying descriptive detail about the clothes worn, the meals eaten and the furnishings of the many rooms in which the narrative is set. Colour, too, is conspicuously absent: Anne Steele's pink ribbons, intended to be alluring to Dr Davies, are a startling exception.

It is worth remembering, of course, that Austen wrote for a social circle never less than genteel, or aspiring to gentility; her contemporary readers were well able to fill in missing details about characters similar to themselves, but readers today might struggle to do so.

Symbolism is a literary device that came into its own in the second half of the nineteenth century. Its use can be said to run counter to the aims of **realism** of which Austen was such a virtuoso exponent, and there is little if any to be found in *Sense and Sensibility*. It is possible, however, that today's readers, with some knowledge of modern psychology, might put an interpretation on Elinor's silence, for instance, or Marianne's tendency to self-destruction, which would see these traits in a symbolic light (see Part Six, Recent Criticism for further comment on this).

PART FOUR

Textual analysis

TEXT 1   (PAGES 183–5)

Those taking part in the following conversation at Mrs Jennings's London house are Elinor Dashwood, Anne and Lucy Steele and Mrs Jennings. The Steeles have recently arrived in London; they have apparently visited the Middletons, where they have been warmly greeted, and now call to pay their respects to Mrs Jennings.

Elinor only was sorry to see them. Their presence always gave her pain, and she hardly knew how to make a very gracious return to the overpowering delight of Lucy in finding her *still* in town.

'I should have been quite disappointed if I had not found you here *still*,' said she repeatedly, with a strong emphasis on the word. 'But I always thought I *should*. I was almost sure you would not leave London yet awhile; though you *told* me, you know, at Barton, that you should not stay above a *month*. But I thought, at the time, that you would most likely change your mind when it came to the point. It would have been such a great pity to have went away before your brother and sister came. And now to be sure you will be in no *hurry* to be gone. I am amazingly glad you did not keep to *your word*.'

Elinor perfectly understood her, and was forced to use all her self-command to make it appear that she did *not*.

'Well, my dear,' said Mrs. Jennings, 'and how did you travel?'

'Not in the stage, I assure you,' replied Miss Steele, with quick exultation; 'we came post all the way, and had a very smart beau to attend us. Dr. Davies was coming to town, and so we thought we'd join him in a post-chaise; and he behaved very genteelly, and paid ten or twelve shillings more than we did.'

'Oh, oh!' cried Mrs Jennings; 'very pretty, indeed! And the Doctor is a single man, I warrant you.'

'There now,' said Miss Steele, affectedly simpering, 'everybody laughs at me so about the Doctor, and I cannot think why. My cousins say they are sure I have made a conquest; but for my part I declare I never think about him from one hour's end to another. "Lord! Here comes your beau, Nancy," my cousin said t'other day, when she saw him crossing the street to the house. "My beau, indeed!" said I—"I cannot think who you mean. The Doctor is no beau of mine." '

'Aye, aye, that is very pretty talking—but it won't do—the Doctor is the man, I see.'

'No, indeed!' replied her cousin, with affected earnestness, 'and I beg you will contradict it, if you ever hear it talked of.'

Mrs. Jennings directly gave her the gratifying assurance that she certainly would *not*, and Miss Steele was made completely happy.

'I suppose you will go and stay with your brother and sister, Miss Dashwood, when they come to town,' said Lucy, returning, after a cessation of hostile hints, to the charge.

'No, I do not think we shall.'

'Oh, yes, I dare say you will.'

Elinor would not humour her by farther opposition.

'What a charming thing it is that Mrs Dashwood can spare you both for so long a time together!'

'Long a time, indeed!' interposed Mrs. Jennings. 'Why, their visit is but just begun!'

Lucy was silenced.

'I am sorry that we cannot see your sister, Miss Dashwood,' said Miss Steele. 'I am sorry she is not well;' for Marianne had left the room on their arrival.

'You are very good. My sister will be equally sorry to miss the pleasure of seeing you; but she has been very much plagued lately with nervous head-akes, which make her unfit for company or conversation.'

'Oh, dear, that is a great pity! But such old friends as Lucy and me!—I think she might see *us*; and I am sure we would not speak a word.'

Elinor, with great civility, declined the proposal. Her sister was perhaps laid down upon the bed, or in her dressing gown, and therefore not able to come to them.

'Oh, if that's all,' cried Miss Steele, 'we can just as well go and see *her*.'

Elinor began to find this impertinence too much for her temper; but she was saved
the trouble of checking it, by Lucy's sharp reprimand, which now, as on many
occasions, though it did not give much sweetness to the manners of one sister, was
of advantage in governing those of the other.

This passage could well be played out as a short scene from a play, the
four characters sitting and, to all appearances, chatting politely. The plot
is not forwarded here, but there is solid confirmation of what is already
known of the Steeles in particular. Elinor, in spite of provocation,
behaves civilly, as would be expected, and the good-natured and not very
perceptive Mrs Jennings does not notice any of the undercurrents at play
between Lucy and Elinor.

Anne and Lucy Steele have obviously come to gloat over
Marianne's disappointment in love, of which they must be aware from
their visit to the Middletons' house, and Lucy also intends to continue
her tormenting of Elinor. The first paragraph is in the **narrator's voice**,
although from Elinor's viewpoint. The words 'sorry' and 'pain' convey her
palpable dismay and contrast with the social hollowness of 'gracious
return' and 'overpowering delight' which follow. Although there is
humour in this juxtaposition, a sombre note – related to Elinor's genuine
misery in this situation – is present, too.

Lucy, of course, has long since recognised Elinor's attachment
to Edward, however much Elinor has tried to disguise her feelings.
When she says, 'I should have been quite disappointed if I had not
found you here *still*,' she and Elinor both know that she is hinting
that of course Elinor would not have gone home yet, when there
was a chance of seeing Edward shortly. Lucy continues with her
cat and mouse tactics, pretending to be pleased but not surprised
to find Elinor still in London. The rash of italics indicates Lucy's
forceful delivery and the boldness of her style, which verges on the
impolite. Apart from her hints about Elinor's need to see Edward,
there are other implications irritating to the reliable Elinor; Lucy
shows no respect for Elinor's integrity when she says, 'I thought...that
you would most likely change your mind when it came to the point' and,
more woundingly still, 'I am amazingly glad that you did not keep
your word.'

Elinor plays her part in this bout of verbal fencing by pretending that she has no idea what lies beneath Lucy's apparently affectionate remarks, but finds it difficult to hide her feelings.

Anne Steele is annoying, too, but in a different way. Silly and more vulgar than her younger sister, she enjoys boasting about the comfortable journey they had to London – not using public transport (the stage coach), but sharing in the private hire of a post-chaise. It is very indelicate of Anne to mention the specific sums paid by themselves and Dr Davies. Mrs Jennings loves a possible romance. The reader learned earlier that now her two daughters were married 'she had nothing to do but to marry all the rest of the world' (p. 32), so she falls in willingly with Anne's nonsense about her 'smart beau'. Of course, in 'affectedly simpering' and protesting so strongly that she is not interested in Dr Davies, Anne is implying quite the opposite – a ploy recognised by Mrs Jennings, who becomes more firmly convinced that there is something between Anne and the doctor.

Lucy's next attack on Elinor's feelings does not last long since, when she suggests that Mrs Dashwood has been without her daughters for an unusually long time, Mrs Jennings – who enjoys their company – exclaims, 'Why, their visit is but just begun!' thus making it impossible for Lucy to continue on that tack.

The visit begins to draw to a close (formal calls were not expected to last for much longer than a quarter of an hour or so) and Anne makes a bid to visit Marianne in her bedroom. (Unlike her socially responsible sister, Marianne is never inclined to endure company she does not like or respect and has disappeared on the arrival of the Steeles.) Although Elinor, too, is suffering wretchedly from unrequited love, she is anxious to protect her sister from their intrusion. Anne's persistence makes this quite difficult. Not recognising Elinor's courteous reply as a refusal, she declares, '…we can just as well go and see *her*.' Today's reader needs to be aware of just how offensive her behaviour is – what sounds perhaps like friendly informality is intolerably intrusive in the Dashwoods' polite society. Even Lucy is embarrassed by her sister's assertive behaviour and rebukes her, offering the narrator an opportunity to end the chapter with the typically excoriating but **balanced** statement that 'though it did not give much sweetness to the manners of one sister, was of advantage in governing those of the other'.

The situation of having to cope with unwanted visitors is one that many readers will have experienced, and Austen gets a full measure of dry humour out of it. Mrs Jennings's inability to recognise the silliness of Anne, or the spitefulness of Lucy, adds a further dimension to Elinor's ordeal. Elinor herself, of course, behaves with almost superhuman civility, given the provocation she undergoes.

The Steeles' lack of good breeding is underlined by Lucy's grammatical slip ('a pity to have went away') and Anne's clumsy and colloquial style. Their emphatic, even noisy, speech is implied by all the words in italics and by the narrator's use of the phrase 'cried Miss Steele' at the end of the passage. Mrs Jennings, too, is a noisy woman, and the reader, always directed to Elinor's viewpoint in this passage, is left in no doubt of how deeply distasteful an encounter this is for her.

TEXT 2 (PAGES 221-3)

Edward Ferrars's long-standing secret engagement to Lucy Steele has been revealed by Anne Steele, and Elinor is at last able to tell Marianne about the distressing news that she has known for four months. Marianne is astonished.

> 'What!—while attending me in all my misery, has this been on your heart?—and I have reproached you for being happy!'—

> 'It was not fit that you should then know how much I was the reverse.'—

> 'Four months!'—cried Marianne again.—'So calm!—so cheerful—how have you been supported?'—

> 'By feeling that I was doing my duty.—My promise to Lucy, obliged me to be secret. I owed it to her, therefore, to avoid giving any hint of the truth; and I owed it to my family and friends, not to create in them a solicitude about me, which it could not be in my power to satisfy.'

> Marianne seemed much struck.—

> 'I have very often wished to undeceive yourself and my mother,' added Elinor; 'and once or twice I have attempted it;—but without betraying my trust, I never could have convinced you.'

'Four months!—and yet you loved him!'—

'Yes. But I did not love only him;—and while the comfort of others was dear to
me, I was glad to spare them from knowing how much I felt. Now, I can think
and speak of it with little emotion.—I would not have you suffer on my account;
for I assure you I no longer suffer materially myself. I have many things to support
me. I am not conscious of having provoked the disappointment by any imprudence
of my own, and I have borne it as much as possible without spreading it farther.—
I acquit Edward of all essential misconduct. I wish him very happy; and I am so
sure of his always doing his duty, that though now he may harbour some regret, in
the end he must become so. Lucy does not want sense, and that is the foundation
upon which every thing good may be built.—And after all, Marianne, after all that
is bewitching in the idea of a single and constant attachment, and all that can be
said of one's happiness depending entirely on any particular person, it is not
meant—it is not fit—it is not possible that it should be so.—Edward will marry
Lucy; he will marry a woman superior in person and understanding to half her sex;
and time and habit will teach him to forget that he ever thought another superior
to *her*.'—

'If such is your way of thinking,' said Marianne, 'if the loss of what is most valued
is so easily to be made up by something else, your resolution, your self-command,
are, perhaps, a little less to be wondered at.—They are brought more within my
comprehension.'

'I understand you.—You do not suppose that I have ever felt much.—For four
months, Marianne, I have had all this hanging on my mind, without being at
liberty to speak of it to a single creature; knowing it would make you and my
mother most unhappy whenever it were explained to you, yet unable to prepare
you for it in the least.—It was told me,—it was in a manner forced on me by the
very person herself, whose prior engagement ruined all my prospects; and told me,
as I thought, with triumph.—This person's suspicions, therefore, I have had to
oppose, by endeavouring to appear indifferent where I have been most deeply
interested;—and it has not been only once;—I have had her hopes and exultation
to listen to again and again.—I have known myself to be divided from Edward for
ever, without hearing one circumstance that could make me less desire the
connection.—Nothing has proved him unworthy; nor has any thing declared him
indifferent to me.—I have had to contend against the unkindness of his sister, and
the insolence of his mother; and have suffered the punishment of an attachment,

without enjoying its advantages.—And all this has been going on at a time, when, as you too well know, it has not been my only unhappiness.—If you can think me capable of ever feeling—surely you may suppose that I have suffered *now*. The composure of mind with which I have brought myself at present to consider the matter, the consolation that I have been willing to admit, have been the effect of constant and painful exertion;—they did not spring up of themselves;—they did not occur to relieve my spirits at first—No, Marianne.—*Then*, if I had not been bound to silence, perhaps nothing could have kept me entirely—not even what I owed to my dearest friends—from openly shewing that I was *very* unhappy.'—

Marianne was quite subdued.—

This passage is central to the analysis of how far Jane Austen ultimately separated sense and sensibility as defining characteristics of her two heroines. At the end of the narrative, the reader learns that Marianne is able to control her sensibility and develop sense; here, the ultra-sensible Elinor reveals her feelings for once – but is this a demonstration of sensibility? This is further discussed in Part Six, Recent Criticism.

Meanwhile, this is a scene of great emotion. Marianne 'seemed much struck' by Elinor's revelations and later 'was quite subdued' – her usual responsiveness silenced by the enormity of what she has heard.

The passage has a shape that allows Elinor's rising emotions full play. First, she gives a clear and rational account of what has happened to her. She no longer suffers much, she says, because: she has done her duty in keeping Lucy's secret; she was glad to be able to spare her family and friends distress; the misfortune is not her fault; Edward has behaved honourably; he can become happy because Lucy does not lack sense; one's happiness should not depend on a particular person; Edward will eventually forget that he loved her more than Lucy.

Elinor's attempt at detachment in this selfless speech is challenged by Austen's punctuation: although no heroine of Austen ever allowed anything to compromise her syntax, her well-chosen sentences are broken by dashes – evidence of a struggle to control emotion. She also makes a brave remark, which challenges Marianne's view of the unique validity of a once and only love, about it not being 'fit' to depend for happiness upon one other person. This interrupts the sequence of her argument about the possibility of Edward finding happiness with Lucy, and seems to show what an effort she is making to speak calmly about such a state of affairs.

Marianne's response shows how little she understands Elinor – or how little Elinor allows others to understand her feelings. Marianne suggests that perhaps Elinor lacks depth of feeling, since she is able to bear the loss of Edward so well. This is the only way she can conceive how Elinor has been able to exercise such self-control and appear 'So calm!—so cheerful!'

This insensitive response provokes Elinor at last to a heartfelt account of what she has been through during the last four months. Her moderate language and rational view of events give place to a passionate explanation of just how wretched she has been. Her vocabulary changes as her emotions prevail for once: for instance, 'I have had all this hanging on my mind, without being at liberty to speak of it to a single creature' is in strong contrast to her previous statement, 'I have very often wished to undeceive yourself and my mother.' Similarly, 'I have known myself to be divided from Edward for ever' needs to be set against what she said earlier about 'happiness depending entirely on any particular person' being not 'fit'. Previously she has spoken as fairly about Lucy as she possibly could, crediting her with that valuable quality – in the terms of the novel – sense. Now her real loathing of the manipulative and spiteful girl comes through, as she refers to her as 'this person', and relives the humiliation of Lucy's 'triumph' and 'exultation' at Elinor's discomfiture, and the fact that she had to endure Lucy's boasting 'again and again'.

As well as directly reproaching Marianne for assuming that she is incapable of suffering, she also implicitly reproaches her for inflicting her own misery on others: while Elinor has been suffering in silence, she has had the additional burden of sharing Marianne's all too apparent grief. That Marianne is 'quite subdued' (i.e. silenced) is evidence that Elinor's outburst has been a revelation to her. For the moment, at least, she recognises the injustice she has done Elinor in supposing her to lack feelings like her own.

TEXT 3   (PAGES 321–3)

The story is ended; after all the difficulties in their way, Elinor and Edward are married and settled in Delaford. Now the pressure is on Marianne to accept her devoted suitor, Colonel Brandon. The

omniscient narrator looks into the future and ties up the novel's final loose ends.

With such a confederacy against her—with a knowledge so intimate of his goodness—with a conviction of his fond attachment to herself, which at last, though long after it was observable to everybody else—burst on her—what could she do?

Marianne Dashwood was born to an extraordinary fate. She was born to discover the falsehood of her own opinions, and to counteract, by her conduct, her most favourite maxims. She was born to overcome an affection formed so late in life as at seventeen, and with no sentiment superior to strong esteem and lively friendship, voluntarily to give her hand to another!—and *that* other, a man who had suffered no less than herself under the event of a former attachment, whom two years before, she had considered too old to be married,—and who still sought the constitutional safe-guard of a flannel waistcoat!

But so it was. Instead of falling a sacrifice to an irresistible passion, as once she had fondly flattered herself with expecting,—instead of remaining even for ever with her mother, and finding her only pleasures in retirement and study, as afterwards in her more calm and sober judgement she had determined on,—she found herself at nineteen, submitting to new attachments, entering on new duties, placed in a new home, a wife, the mistress of a family, and the patroness of a village.

Colonel Brandon was now as happy, as all those who best loved him, believed he deserved to be;—in Marianne he was consoled for every past affliction;—her regard and her society restored his mind to animation, and his spirits to cheerfulness; and that Marianne found her own happiness in forming his, was equally the persuasion and the delight of each observing friend. Marianne could never love by halves; and her whole heart became, in time, as much devoted to her husband, as it had once been to Willoughby.

Willoughby could not hear of her marriage without a pang; and his punishment was soon afterwards complete in the voluntary forgiveness of Mrs. Smith, who, by stating his marriage with a woman of character, as the source of her clemency, gave him reason for believing that had he behaved with honour towards Marianne, he might at once have been happy and rich. That his repentance of misconduct, which thus brought its own punishment, was sincere, need not be doubted;—nor that he long thought of Colonel Brandon with envy, and of Marianne with regret.

But that he was for ever inconsolable, that he fled from society, or contracted an habitual gloom of temper, or died of a broken heart, must not be depended on—for he did neither. He lived to exert, and frequently to enjoy himself. His wife was not always out of humour, nor his home always uncomfortable; and in his breed of horses and dogs, and in sporting of every kind, he found no inconsiderable degree of domestic felicity.

For Marianne, however—in spite of his incivility in surviving her loss—he always retained that decided regard which interested him in everything that befell her, and made her his secret standard of perfection in woman;—and many a rising beauty would be slighted by him in after days as bearing no comparison with Mrs. Brandon.

Mrs. Dashwood was prudent enough to remain at the cottage, without attempting a removal to Delaford; and fortunately for Sir John and Mrs. Jennings, when Marianne was taken from them, Margaret had reached an age highly suitable for dancing, and not very ineligible for being supposed to have a lover.

Between Barton and Delaford, there was that constant communication which strong family affection would naturally dictate;—and among the merits and the happiness of Elinor and Marianne, let it not be ranked as the least considerable, that though sisters, and living almost within sight of each other, they could live without disagreement between themselves, or producing coolness between their husbands.

In the formal **closure**, typical of Jane Austen's style, the author has to persuade the reader that her second heroine's emotional adventures have a happy outcome, and to outline for her a rosy future to parallel that of her sister. This the narrator does by taking on a worldly and humorous approach to the pangs of teenage disappointed love, suggesting that they are eminently curable, and that the rash and romantic opinions of the young are likely to be moderated within the span of a few years. With heavy **irony**, the narrator claims that 'Marianne Dashwood was born to an extraordinary fate', meaning, of course, the reverse – that Marianne's development of a more balanced view of life and love is a commonplace of growing up. Gentle fun is made of Marianne's discovering 'the falsehood of her own opinions' – finding that her views are not immutable, as she had once imagined, and that it is perfectly possible to find another love, having lost the first at seventeen. Edged towards acceptance of Colonel Brandon by 'a confederacy' of friends and family, she revises her passionate concept of love, which had been so disastrous. She marries Brandon in spite of what she had once considered to be his near-senility and his liking for a flannel waistcoat. Her acceptance of him on the basis of 'no sentiment superior to strong esteem and lively friendship' implies the narrator's belief that there could be no better foundation for marriage.

The use in the third paragraph of the helpless-sounding 'she found herself' suggests the inevitability of marriage for a girl like Marianne. It also hints that in conforming to what society wants, she has given up the fierce and difficult individuality with which she faced the world at seventeen.

If a moral tone is to be detected behind the narrator's satirical praise of 'esteem and friendship' as the basis for marriage, it is evident too in the paragraph about Colonel Brandon: 'Marianne found her own happiness in forming his' is a comment on wifely duties. Her reward was that 'her whole heart became, in time, as much devoted to her husband, as it had once been to Willoughby'. Whether or not the reader is convinced that this is the best outcome to be wished for Marianne is a controversial matter, and there is further comment in Part Six, Critical History.

The fate of the dashing Willoughby is dealt with at some length. He is a strong presence in the narrative, succeeding not only in bowling over Marianne, but – even after the revelations of his perfidy – in persuading Elinor to forgive him. In spite of the formal settling of all the main characters' futures, the narrative undercuts any lack of **realism** associated with romantic fiction by its satiric tone and shrewd understanding of human nature. A romantic work would end, the narrator implies, with Willoughby 'for ever inconsolable', or having 'fled from society' and 'contracted an habitual gloom of temper' or even having 'died of a broken heart'. But *Sense and Sensibility* more resembles a **comedy of manners** (see Part Five, Literary Background). The realism of Austen's work requires a more down-to-earth analysis, and the narrator, having discarded the options of the arch-romantic, moves quickly to acknowledging that the villain of the piece 'found no inconsiderable domestic felicity'. He is an energetic figure, who 'lived to exert, and frequently to enjoy himself', a recognition of the sporting and other outdoor activities that were open to men, but not to women, at the time.

None the less, Willoughby heard of Marianne's marriage with 'a pang', and the genuine depth of his feeling for her is conveyed by his interest in news of her and in that he 'made her his secret standard of perfection in woman', the latter in recognition of her physical beauty.

Mrs Dashwood continues to live at Barton Cottage, and Margaret soon moves into the gap left in Barton Park society by Marianne's marriage. It is clear that Marianne's contempt for Sir John and Mrs Jennings is now in the past, and she, like the reader, has discovered in them a warmth and kindness that are more important than their lack of social graces. Mrs Dashwood is described as 'prudent enough' to stay at the cottage, presumably a reference to not interfering in her married daughters' lives, and perhaps an acknowledgement of Barton Park's usefulness in providing opportunities for her youngest daughter to find a husband.

Finally, the narrator describes the friendly relations that continue between Barton and Delaford, with much visiting, and there is special commendation for the tact and delicacy of Elinor and Marianne. Avoiding the unhappy and quarrelsome situations of John and Fanny Dashwood and the Robert Ferrars (savagely satirised on p. 320), Elinor and Marianne are able to maintain loving and harmonious relations between not only themselves but also their husbands.

PART FIVE

BACKGROUND

JANE AUSTEN'S LIFE

EARLY DAYS

Jane Austen was born on 16 December 1775 in her father's country rectory in Steventon, Hampshire. She was the sixth child and second daughter of the Reverend George Austen and his wife, Cassandra (née Leigh). There was to be one more son.

George Austen's grandfather had been a wealthy cloth merchant who fell on hard times; his widow and children, including George's father, William, had to leave their Horsmonden manor house and remained the poor relations in the Austen family. However, William became a surgeon and, with the help of a prosperous relative, had his son, Jane Austen's father, educated at Oxford. The support shown by the wealthy towards struggling members of the family (not unusual at that time) is paralleled perhaps in Sir John Middleton's timely offer of a house to his needy cousin, Mrs Dashwood.

Jane Austen's mother was the daughter of a Church of England clergyman with aristocratic connections, and niece of Theophilus Leigh, Master of Balliol (an Oxford College) for fifty years. The widespread family network, which covered a good deal of England and beyond, formed the setting for Austen's life. The large families of the period and the many early deaths, which resulted in second and third marriages and more sets of step-relations (as in *Sense and Sensibility*), meant that family connections – kept up by correspondence and visits – could be very extensive.

Jane Austen's parents ran a small boarding school for boys at their home in the rectory, where their sons were educated until they were at least twelve. Young Jane and her slightly older sister, Cassandra, would have been very much aware of the boys' noisy presence; the boarders, aged up to fourteen or fifteen, were always there, except for breaks at Christmas and in the summer.

Jane had five brothers: the eldest, James, followed his father to Oxford and succeeded him as rector of Steventon. Her second brother,

George, who did not live at home, suffered from an undiagnosed illness, which afflicted him mentally and physically all his life. The next brother, Edward, was adopted by wealthy but childless relatives, the Knights, and inherited Godmersham Park in Kent. At that time parents of numerous offspring often thought it an advantage for a child to be adopted or brought up by wealthier relatives – as in Austen's *Mansfield Park*, where Fanny Price is brought up by the Bertrams. Henry Austen, the favourite brother, became a young man of great charm and various careers: he was first a captain in the militia, later a London banker and finally, after his bank crashed, was ordained and given a clerical living by his rich brother, now Edward Knight. The other brothers, Frank and Charles, had successful naval careers, both rising to become admirals.

Jane's only sister, Cassandra, was about two years older than Jane, and they were always devoted to each other. Since the boys' school in the rectory was seen as inappropriate for the girls' education, they were sent away to a small Oxford boarding school when Jane was seven. This school removed to Southampton, where Cassandra and Jane became ill with an infectious fever and were eventually taken home. There are few cheerful accounts of boarding schools of that period, and conditions were often harsh. Nevertheless, the girls were soon sent off again, this time to a school in Reading, where lessons were short and free time was long. When Jane was eleven, her boarding school life ended and she went home, where her education continued on an informal basis: she studied French and Italian, learned to play the piano, and continued for the rest of her life the wide reading that had always been central to her tastes (see Literary Background for her favourite authors).

ADULT LIFE

In 1801, the Reverend George Austen retired with his wife and daughters to lodgings in Bath. Jane, very fond of the Steventon Rectory, fainted in the kitchen when she heard they were to leave their home. She disliked Bath but enjoyed the summer travelling the family undertook to seaside places. There is a story, recounted by Cassandra in old age, that in one of the towns they visited in Devon her sister Jane developed a romantic interest in a young man who showed some signs of courting her. But before the possibility of another summer meeting, they learned of his death. Claire Tomalin, one of Austen's biographers, identifies another possible attachment that came to nothing: while Jane was still at Steventon, she met a young Irishman, Tom Lefroy, a relative of her brother James's in-laws. They met at a ball at Manydown, the manor home of friends, the Bigg-Withers. Jane wrote several letters to Cassandra about this delightful young man, with whom she had much in common, including a shared interest in Henry Fielding's *Tom Jones* (1749). He agreed later in life that he had been in love with Jane Austen. However, at the time of their meetings, when Jane was twenty, young Lefroy had to make his way in the world, and must have been steered away by his family from involvement with a clergyman's penniless daughter. Jane did not behave as rashly as Marianne did with Willoughby, but, says her biographer, she made no secret of her attraction to Tom Lefroy.

After leaving Steventon, Jane and Cassandra spent much of their time on visits to friends and relatives. In 1802, for instance, they spent eight weeks in Kent with their brother Charles and, on returning to pay visits in Hampshire, were invited to spend several weeks at Manydown. Here, Harris Bigg-Wither proposed to Jane, whom he had known all his life. She accepted, amid general approval. In time she would have become the mistress of a large house and estate – the kind of happy ending she planned for her heroines. But doubts crept in; next morning she told Harris she could not marry him, and left at once with Cassandra for Bath to avoid further embarrassment. Jane was not, after all, to have the usual young woman's career of marriage and children. Her adventure in life was to be a very different one: no husband, but a gift for friendship; no children, but her novels, which she described as such. When she saw *Sense and Sensibility* finally in print, she said, 'I can no more forget it, than a mother can forget her sucking child', and *Pride and Prejudice* was her 'darling child'.

Cassandra, meanwhile, had been engaged to a naval officer, who died of fever in the West Indies in 1797. She and Jane drew even closer and – rather too quickly, it was thought – gave up dancing and other pleasures of youth, and took on the characteristics of old maids. After 1805, the year of their father's death, there was a period of some hardship for George Austen's widow and daughters, as there was no church pension for them at that time. The loss of her sympathetic father was a great blow to Jane, and life became very unsettled: they had no real home of their own, and spent the years until 1809 on an endless round of visits. Then, at last, the two sisters and their mother were offered a house by their wealthiest brother, Edward – a rescue similar to that of Sir John's to Mrs Dashwood and daughters. The house, called a 'cottage', was probably a one-time posting inn, with six bedrooms, gardens and outbuildings, and was situated at Chawton, in the Austens' home county of Hampshire.

Jane, previously depressed and without a regular pattern of life, had written nothing for several years. Now, happily settled at Chawton, she was to write again and see her work published. She had no room of her own, but cheerfully worked on a table in the drawing-room, where she could cover up her papers in the event of a visitor calling.

Her last years before her illness and death were busy and contented. Her large family and her friends experienced good and bad fortune, of course, and she shared their happiness and grief. Chawton society was limited, but she continued her visits – especially to Henry in London, where she enjoyed the theatres and shops. She died while in Winchester on 18 July 1817, and was buried in the cathedral, where her memorial recognises her Christian qualities. It is often said that no mention is made on her tombstone of her life's work, but this is belied by the reference to 'the extraordinary endowments of her mind'.

Writing

Apart from her brother James's writing successes – he was published in his own magazine, *The Loiterer* (1789–91), and elsewhere – Jane's mother, Cassandra, was also a talented writer. In spite of the daunting duties involved in running a large household and school, she sometimes dashed off humorous verses.

Jane herself was writing by the age of twelve: her recent biographer, Claire Tomalin, suggests in *Jane Austen: A Life* (1997) that these early stories are influenced by the boys' humour with which she was so familiar at home. In *Jack and Alice*, dedicated to her brother Francis, there are jokes about drunkenness, food, violent death and accidents, speculation about adult behaviour and rude remarks about personal appearances.

Tomalin writes: 'Jane Austen was a tough and unsentimental child, drawn to rude, anarchic imaginings and black jokes' (p. 30). It may well be said that she retained that tough and unsentimental approach in her adult work: her **comedies of manners,** however conventionally happy their endings, have a hard, shrewd core to them.

At the age of fourteen, she dedicated *Love and Friendship* to her glamorous cousin Eliza, who had married a French count. This **epistolary** work, not unrelated to *Elinor and Marianne*, and therefore to *Sense and Sensibility,* hilariously sent up the contemporary taste for sensibility. It is memorable particularly for an image of the two heroines taking it in turns to indulge their sensibilities as they 'fainted alternately on a sofa'.

While still in her teens, Jane changed her subject matter and her range increased: her comical *History of England* (dated 26 November 1791) is full of family jokes and references. *Lesley Castle* (1792), another heartless epistolary story, focuses on a huge wedding banquet and the provision of food for it. This is a scandalous tale of child abandonment, adultery and conversion to Roman Catholicism, topics that her Church of England father was able to appreciate in a spirit of literary criticism. He was a great admirer and encourager of his daughter's aspirations, taking care that she always had paper – then an expensive item – to write on.

Probably without her knowledge, her father sent her novel *First Impressions* (1797) to a publisher, who promptly turned it down – a serious misjudgement, since it was later published as *Pride and Prejudice.* An earlier work, *Lady Susan* (1789–9), later rewritten as *Northanger Abbey,* but not published until after Jane's death, was bought for publication in 1803. She was rewriting *Sense and Sensibility* in 1797–8, but it was not until 1811, when Jane was thirty-five, that it was published as her first novel. This proved to be a success, and was followed in 1813 by *Pride and Prejudice.*

Jane's regular writing activity stopped abruptly in 1805, probably due to her father's death. (She abandoned, unfinished, a novel called *The Watsons* in that year.) Once settled again in a permanent home, and no doubt buoyed up by successful publication, she began *Mansfield Park* in 1811, *Emma* in 1814, *Persuasion* in 1816, and *Sanditon,* unfinished at her death, in 1817. Her novels were published anonymously, but her authorship became an open secret, with her readership extending to court circles: the Prince Regent, whom Jane detested, let it be known that he would allow a work to be dedicated to him. Jane followed his wishes reluctantly.

LITERARY BACKGROUND

Jane Austen's style owes most to the reasoned **classicism** of the eighteenth century; her themes – love, marriage, betrayal and loyalty – are traditional; her **ironic** stance delivers her comedies in the form of acute commentaries on contemporary mores.

Generally, the prevailing **balanced** prose style of the so-called Age of Reason is what Jane Austen has adapted to her narrative purpose. The weightiness of the style is particularly effective in its incongruity when applied to **satire**. A well-known example is Alexander Pope's *The Rape of the Lock* (1712), in which the poet's **mock heroic** style underlines the trivialities with which he is dealing, and this is also the style of Henry Fielding's mid-century political plays, moderated into something more suited to narrative in his novels, which he described as 'comic epics'.

The eighteenth century saw the birth of the English novel in its recognisable form. Among those known as the 'fathers' of this form – and admired by Jane Austen – were Fielding, whose *Tom Jones* (1749) was a particular favourite, and Samuel Richardson, whose extended **epistolary novels** – the best known is *Pamela, or Virtue Rewarded* (1740) – were models for some of Austen's **juvenilia**, as well as *Sense and Sensibility*, which began life as the epistolary novel *Elinor and Marianne*. Austen also enjoyed – and learned from – the novels of Fanny Burney (1752–1840), and the essayist and lexicographer Samuel Johnson (1709–84), whose style she much admired. Favourite poets were George Crabbe (1754–1832), William Cowper (1731–1800) and particularly Walter Scott (1771–1832), who are all mentioned with approval in connection with the heroines of her novels.

Although her work was not published until 1811, by the end of the eighteenth century Austen had joined the proliferating novelists of the period, several of whom were women. But by this time classicism, which had long been the major identifying mode of the arts generally, had given way to **Romanticism** – and reason to sensibility.

ROMANTICISM AND SENSIBILITY

A somewhat loose term (as is classicism), Romanticism values emotion, individualism and concepts of freedom; the style is intense and imaginative; the landscape, the power of nature and the supernatural are central. **Sensibility** was the quality most admired in its heroes and heroines, who featured in what was known as the **sentimental novel**; they demonstrated a sense of strict personal morality and honour, accompanied by intensified feelings and kind-heartedness. The arch-hero of what became a popular **genre**, with many practitioners, was Harley, the central character of H. Mackenzie's *The Man of Feeling* (1771). Harley is presented in a series of episodes in which he attempts to help the unfortunate, somewhat tearfully maintains his integrity, but loses his lover and is a worldly failure.

Another influential hero of great sensibility was Goethe's Werther, who appeared in an English translation of the German novel *Sorrows of Young Werther* in 1779. It was a cult work, and Wertherism became widespread in Europe. The hero kills himself as the result of a hopeless love, and disappointed love and suicide became linked in the Romantic novel. Marianne in *Sense and Sensibility* shows signs of this desperate response to disappointment in love, collapsing into a self-induced and nearly fatal illness.

In the 1790s, when Austen was first writing about the perils of sensibility in the form of *Elinor and Marianne,* the topic was already in the public consciousness. Mary Wollstonecraft's *Vindication of the Rights of Women* (1792) caused a furore: she was referred to, for instance, as 'a hyena in petticoats' because of her radical approach to the traditional role of women. Biographer Claire Tomalin points out that there are parallels between Wollstonecraft's own 'outspokenness, refusal to conform to social rules and attempted self-destruction when love fails' and Marianne Dashwood's character. She does not go so far as to say that Marianne was modelled on Wollstonecraft, but points out that the denigrated writer's story was well known to the Austen family through a mutual friend.

However, Mary Wollstonecraft was actually as opposed in her way to the notion of sensibility as Austen was. She felt that women, traditionally the weaker sex, used their supposed sensibility to maintain their right to dependence upon the stronger male, a situation from which they should break free.

While sensibility was a central feature of Romanticism, it was only one aspect of what was a widespread movement, the tenets of which were followed in a spectrum of the arts stretching from poetry to the appreciation of the **picturesque** in landscape (see Social Background). The Romantic **Gothic** novel was very popular, its chief exponents towards the close of the century being Matthew 'Monk' Lewis (1775–1818), William Beckford (1759–1844) and Ann Radcliffe (1764–1823), most famous for *The Mysteries of Udolpho* (1794). In these over-heated works, terror, passion and madness reigned amid abductions to foreign castles, rapes, fires and tempests. These wild matters were not for Jane Austen, an early **realist**, although she used the genre to satirical purpose in *Northanger Abbey*: the heroine, Catherine Morland – steeped in Romantic Gothic novels – finally realises that it is not in the works of Radcliffe that 'human nature, at least in the midland counties of England, was to be looked for'.

THE COMEDY OF MANNERS

If Radcliffe's work is satirised in *Northanger Abbey*, other women writers were read with approval. The novels of 'manners' by Fanny Burney, who moved in courtly circles, and of Maria Edgeworth (1768–1849) are identified as worthy examples. Some of Burney's older women characters in *Cecilia* (1782) and *Evelina* (1778) make embarrassingly vulgar remarks, rather as Mrs Jennings does in *Sense and Sensibility*.

Although the novel was an increasingly popular form, it was frequently dismissed by the serious-minded as frivolous. In *Northanger Abbey* Austen's narrator makes a well-known defence of the novel, describing it as 'only some work in which the greatest powers of the human mind are displayed, in which the most thorough knowledge of human nature, the happiest delineation of its varieties, the liveliest effusions of wit and humour, are conveyed to the world in the best chosen language'.

Influenced as she was by admired writers, particularly of the eighteenth century, but reacting against the excesses of Romanticism, Jane Austen's work remains unique. With no need for wider literary ambitions and with a highly sophisticated writing technique, she is perhaps the first virtuoso of the novel form.

SOCIAL BACKGROUND

REVOLUTION AND WARS

Jane Austen adhered to the advice she gave her would-be novelist niece, to limit the scope of her characters and settings to a few families in a country village. It was not her intention to deal with a wider horizon, although she has often been criticised for ignoring the events of the day (see Part Six, Critical History).

Certainly, she lived through turbulent times: the American War of Independence was fought during her childhood, and the French Revolution – the clearest manifestation of **Romantic** philosophy – began when she was in her teens. England's subsequent wars with France and French allies continued almost until the end of Austen's life. There was an Irish rebellion and wars were fought in India from the end of the eighteenth century. Although war is not a theme that interested Austen as a novelist, many of her characters are soldiers or sailors: in *Sense and Sensibility* there is a glancing reference to the wars in India, when it is mentioned that Colonel Brandon had exchanged his posting there with another officer in order to return to England.

Wars and other international troubles did not impinge a great deal on the everyday lives of country gentlemen and their families, although wages fell drastically for agricultural workers. As always in times of war, fortunes were made and lost among the rich, but none of the wealthy characters in *Sense and Sensibility* appears to suffer financial hardship. John Dashwood's many complaints about his imaginary straitened circumstances are to do with the lavish scale of his family's life.

Fashionable life

Fashion in all things was led by the Prince of Wales, later the Prince Regent. In spite of his political shortcomings and notorious private life, he left a legacy of what is called Regency style, which is marked particularly by changes in architecture and landscape gardening, in dress and in public entertainment.

While still Prince of Wales, and with his dandyish friend 'Beau' Brummel, he made it essential for the fashionable to spend time each year at the spa town of Bath, taking advantage of the medicinal waters, promenading and attending concerts, balls and lectures. Jane Austen's father retired there in 1801, and the writer disliked the place, preferring the less intense pleasures of Cheltenham when she felt the need to take a 'cure'. Patronised by the Prince, seaside towns, such as Brighton – where he had the famous Pavilion built – became fashionable for the first time. Horse racing had been a royal hobby since the days of Charles II, and the Prince Regent owned some of the finest horses in the country. Ladies rode for their health: in *Sense and Sensibility* Marianne is delighted to be offered the use of a horse by Willoughby. Elinor persuades her of the impropriety of accepting, or at least of the unmanageable expense of stabling and the necessary addition of another horse and attendant, since young ladies did not ride alone.

Dress

In the aftermath of the French Revolution, dress changed dramatically: the extravagant styles of the eighteenth century gave way to a simple elegance, or even to austerity in those who wished to recognise the principles of the Revolution. Some members of the upper classes thought it prudent to modify their style of dress to avoid any affinity with those who had been violently overthrown in France. Men no longer wore wigs or powdered their hair; buckles and fancy trimmings gave way to an elegant outline; and black or dark colours were favoured. Dress etiquette was strict, however, and the arbiters of taste were the Prince and 'Beau' Brummel.

Young women, such as Jane and Cassandra Austen – and Austen's heroines – constantly risked chills, since the neoclassical style adopted was typically a loose, flimsy, light-coloured dress, caught in below the breasts, which were generously exposed. It is therefore unsurprising when Marianne catches a cold in the wet grounds of Cleveland. Older women wore the same style, but usually in a more substantial fabric. At evening balls or public events a long feather or two arranged above a light turban – or some variation on this theme – was usual. Bonnets were daytime wear. As with men, there was a striking change in hairstyle. Women wore their hair up, usually with a curled fringe around the forehead (as in the well-known watercolour of Jane Austen by her sister). Gone were the long tresses and ringlets that had hung down around the head; in what seemed to some a macabre reference to the victims of the guillotine, the neck was left bare.

Domestic life

The aristocracy remained a small, fairly impenetrable élite, who often lived very splendidly, employing regiments of servants and estate workers. For the gentry, to the lower reaches of which Jane Austen's family belonged, domestic work was also greatly eased by the employment of servants. Norland and Barton Park, homes of the prosperous gentry, obviously have large numbers of servants, although they are not identified. Even the less than prosperous Dashwoods at Barton Cottage have three servants – a man, Thomas, and two women.

    With servants to do everything practical, the ladies of the house, in particular, were left with many idle hours. The Dashwoods' industry in applying themselves to reading and other interests is considered remarkable by Sir John Middleton. Men had interests in their estates and, like Willoughby, in energetic outdoor activities. Their wives and sisters led a mainly indoor life, especially in a bad winter when, as Jane Austen wrote in a letter, it was not fit for a 'female foot' to venture out, although the well-booted men could do so. The visits to stay with distant relatives and friends, or local trips to neighbours, were a central part of Austen's life, as they are for many of her characters.

'PLEASURE GROUNDS', GARDENS AND THE PICTURESQUE

Developments in landscape gardening had continued throughout the eighteenth century, with a move away from the formally structured layouts of earlier years. The leading exponent of what was known as the 'Naturalist' school was 'Capability' Brown (1716–83): he abhorred straight lines and level areas, and his work is typified by curved paths, undulating grassy areas and irregularly shaped lakes. 'Follies' – outdoor ornamental buildings, such as temples, grottoes, or towers – were carefully placed to re-create something approaching the calmly classical landscapes of Nicolas Poussin (1594–1665). By the beginning of the nineteenth century the even newer **picturesque** features were introduced by modernising owners of large houses and gardens. These 'improvements' – always an ambivalent term in Austen's work – included the addition of dramatic features, such as artificial waterfalls, hillocks and imported craggy rocks, often in imitation of admired landscapes, such as the bandit-ridden Italian terrains of artist Salvator Rosa (1615–73). This style is mockingly referred to by Edward Ferrars (p. 85) in his teasing of Marianne about taste in landscape,

Landscape gardener Humphry Repton (1752–1818) was the leading practitioner and exponent of the picturesque; others, such as the writer William Gilpin (1724–1804), who seems to be referred to in Volume I, Chapter 18, laid down rules for the correct appreciation of the style. The Dashwood sisters and Edward Ferrars are all aware of the somewhat pretentious nature of this aesthetic theory, and in the chapter just mentioned Edward enjoys himself with some satirical comments about the picturesque.

MARRIAGE

For most women of the class with which Austen is concerned there were no prospects but marriage and the raising of children. Parents of daughters, such as Mrs Dashwood (or Mrs Bennet in *Pride and Prejudice*), have a heavy responsibility to see their children married. Refusing a 'good' offer of marriage (like Fanny's refusal of Crawford in *Mansfield Park*, or Jane's own refusal of Harris Bigg-Wither) could be considered reckless, since an unmarried woman would be dependent on support from relatives, as Jane Austen was for much of her life.

The only acceptable alternative was to become a governess – an often uncomfortable position in which genteel status was in peril. Needless to say, Austen's own career was unusual, and only just becoming respectable, so she took the precaution of publishing her work anonymously.

The church

Church-going had diminished in the eighteenth century – the Age of Reason – and absentee clergymen had been easy subjects for **satire**. The events surrounding the French Revolution effected a change of heart, and church-going resumed a central place in society at the end of the century. Reforms were afoot: although in 1780 a quarter of the 10,000 parishes in England had no resident parson, a Bill of 1808 required all clergymen to live in their parishes, an obligation that Edward Ferrars seems intent on fulfilling at Delaford, although he would doubtless have had a very low-paid curate to assist him.

By this time, there were fewer impoverished clergy; Jane Austen's own father had a comfortable income (although the Church later made no provision for his widow and unmarried daughters).

Edward Ferrars' preparation for ordination at Oxford is very low key in *Sense and Sensibility*, but Jane Austen rarely dwells on men's work, and there is no reason to suppose that she did not consider his vocation a serious matter. She herself was a traditional member of the Church of England and was apparently not drawn to the evangelical movements, such as Quakerism and Methodism, which arose at the end of the eighteenth century. She wrote to her sister after a church service with evangelical overtones that she did not much like the new sermons: 'They are fuller of Regeneration and Conversion than ever.'

PART SIX

CRITICAL HISTORY &
BROADER PERSPECTIVES

EARLY RESPONSES

Sense and Sensibility was published privately towards the end of 1811. The publisher, Thomas Egerton, was indifferent to the merits of the novel, and printing costs were paid by Austen's brother, James, and his wife Eliza, cousin and close friend of Jane. The three-volume novel of probably no more than 1,000 copies cost 15 shillings (75 pence in modern money, but an expensive item at the time), and sold out by mid-1813. Jane Austen's profit was £140 – the first money she earned for herself.

The *British Critic* and the *Critical Review* wrote approvingly of the novel in 1812, the latter commenting that it was well written and 'the characters are in genteel life, naturally drawn, and judiciously supported. The incidents are probable, and highly pleasing, and interesting; the conclusion such as the reader must wish it should be.'

Unperceptive and anodyne as it was, this recommendation would have helped the novel to find acceptance among those still ambivalent about the genre's status and morality. However, it was taken up enthusiastically by a more worldly and influential circle. Biographer Claire Tomalin (see Further Reading) says that Lady Bessborough, a friend of the dramatist Sheridan and of the Prince of Wales, was greatly amused by the novel, although she complained that it ended 'stupidly'. Sixteen-year-old Princess Charlotte (daughter of the Prince of Wales) wrote in a letter that 'Maryanne & me are very alike in *disposition*, that certainly I am not so good, the same imprudence, &c however remain very like'.

Austen was a great admirer of the historical novels and verse of Sir Walter Scott and, although he did not mention *Sense and Sensibility* specifically, he offered modest praise for the **realism** of her work generally in the *Quarterly Review* (Vol. xiv, 1815): 'The narrative of all her novels is composed of such common occurrences as may have fallen under the observation of most folks; and her *dramatis personae* conduct themselves upon the motives and principles which the readers may recognize as ruling their own and that of most of their acquaintances.'

Later, after Austen's death – although still referring to her as 'that young lady' – he came to a greater appreciation of her talent, directed as it was towards such a different narrative goal from his own. In an entry in his diary for March 1826, Scott wrote of Jane Austen:

> [She] has a talent for describing the involvements and feelings and characters of ordinary life, which is to me the most wonderful that I have ever met with. The Big Bow-Wow strain I can do myself like any now going; but the exquisite touch which renders common-place things and characters interesting from the truth of the description and sentiment is denied to me.

It was the publication of nephew James-Edward Austen-Leigh's memoirs of Jane Austen in 1870 that led to her wider popularity and prompted much more critical interest. By the end of the nineteenth century, many publishers had produced editions of her major novels, which have never subsequently been out of print.

Throughout most of their critical history the works of Jane Austen have tended to generate a polarisation of views, with supporters and detractors lining up against each other. The nineteenth century saw her attacked by the popular novelist Charlotte Brontë (1816–55) and the poet Elizabeth Barrett Browning (1806–61) for what they saw as a limiting lack of emotion or passion in her writing; in the United States, Austen's work was spurned by Mark Twain (1835–1910) and Ralph Waldo Emerson (1803–82) as tedious. At the beginning of the twentieth century, D.H. Lawrence (1885–1930) found her novels 'snobbish', among other things. Some of Jane Austen's supporters have included the novelist George Eliot (1819–80) and her partner, the writer G.H. Lewes (1817–78), who admired Austen but saw her work as likely to appeal to an intellectual élite within 'a small circle of cultivated minds'. Novelists as diverse as Henry James (1843–1916) and Rudyard Kipling (1865–1936) have been admirers of Jane Austen; the latter wrote a short story, *The Janeites* (1936), which identifies and celebrates an Austen cult.

A now little-known novelist, Julia Kavanagh, perceptively identified in 1862 an almost tragic strain in Austen's comedies, which is particularly evident in her two darker novels, *Sense and Sensibility* and *Mansfield Park*: 'If we look into the shrewdness and quiet satire of her stories, we shall find a much keener sense of disappointment than joy fulfilled.'

Certainly, many readers and critics have demurred at the fate of Marianne, who docilely gives up dreams of passion for decent but dull Colonel Brandon. This acceptance that the humdrum may not exclude the possibility of happiness, and may indeed nourish it, is closely linked with the overt theme of the novel – the opposed qualities of sense and **sensibility**. On the face of it, the theme is clearly expressed, with considerate and socially aware Elinor representing worthy sense, and headstrong, over-emotional Marianne representing dangerous sensibility. Critic Andrew Wright, in *Jane Austen's Novels* (1953, p. 93) points out that this is acceptable only

> from a narrowly moralistic point of view. But on a higher level the book contains the germ of divided vision: Elinor and Marianne are in fact twin heroines, each embodying a mode of existence which is desirable, but which contradicts the other. And the grand irony is that Elinor and Marianne virtually interchange their positions (although there are many modifications along the way): Marianne, it is quite clear, does gradually acquire sense; but it is also true that Elinor becomes increasingly sensitive as the book progresses. So the two elder Dashwood sisters function not as mere allegorical figures but as ironic symbols.

Wright sums up his account by saying that 'the "lesson" of the book is that neither mode is adequate, each contradicts the other – and there is no happy medium' (ibid., p. 99). This view of the nature of these contradictions is supported by Margaret Kirkham in *Jane Austen, Feminism and Fiction* (1983), although she believes it is the novel's structure, with its device of two heroines, that causes unresolvable difficulties: 'The schema entailed the showing up of one sister against the other, rather than the endorsements of their superior judgement in the face of prejudice and error in less sensitive and sensible people. It did not therefore permit the adequate representation of a single heroine with a good head and a sound heart.' (p. 87)

Commentaries pre-dating 1938 by those mentioned above and many others are collected in Brian Southam's comprehensive work *Jane Austen: The Critical Heritage* (see Further Reading).

In spite of some critical reservations, and a widening recognition of the complexities of the sense versus sensibility theme, the supportive critical comments mentioned earlier have on the whole been directed towards the delights of Austen's text and the effects of her characterisation on readers' susceptibilities. More recent developments in literary criticism have focused on different cultural insights into her work.

The work of many contemporary critics follows a reaction against the so-called **New Criticism** of the earlier part of the twentieth century. The supporters of the New Criticism stressed the aesthetic inviolability of a work of art – that is to say, a poem should be studied as a poem, a novel as a novel, and not for other than aesthetic reasons. Some of the critics who have rejected the aesthetic constraints of the New Criticism are identified by David Lodge in *After Bakhtin* (1990, Chapter 8) as discovering a classic **realist** text, such as *Sense and Sensibility*, or any other one of Austen's novels, to be 'an instrument of ideology, a genre founded on bad faith, on the pretence that bourgeois culture is "natural", using the dominance of the authorial voice...to limit meaning in the interests of control, repression and privilege'. He also agrees that Jane Austen accepted 'the existence of class society (although she did not see it as fixed or static), that she subscribed to the Christian-humanist notion of the autonomy and responsibility of the individual self, and that her novels unequivocally endorse certain values and reject others'. Having accepted the validity of this Marxist argument as a description of what underlies Austen's view of the world, Lodge goes on to say that he does not believe that these are grounds for the condemnation of a novelist. He argues for a return to 'a reaffirmation of the writer's creative and communicative power' and deplores what he sees as 'a barrier of non-comprehension between academic and non-academic discussion of literature'.

However, the concept of the classic realist novel as 'an instrument of ideology' is explored by many critics. *Jane Austen and the War of Ideas* (1975) by Marilyn Butler was particularly influential, and she sees *Sense and Sensibility* as an example of literary **anti-jacobinism** – namely a novel that challenged the radical views of Romanticism and revolution. Therefore, Butler sees Austen's novel as unequivocal in its intention to attack the cult of individualism that manifested itself in the character of Marianne:

Jane Austen's version of 'sensibility' – that is, individualism, or the worship of self, in various familiar guises – is as harshly dealt with here as anywhere in the anti-jacobin tradition. Even without the melodramatic political subplot of many anti-jacobin novels, Mrs Ferrars's London is recognizably a sketch of the anarchy that follows the loss of all values but self-indulgence. In the opening chapters especially, where Marianne is the target of criticism, 'sensibility' means sentimental (or revolutionary) idealism, which Elinor counters with her sceptical or pessimistic view of man's nature. (p. 194)

SILENCES

To some **post-structuralist** critics, what Jane Austen does not say is even more revealing than what she does. The examination of 'gaps' in the overall narrative is one aspect of **deconstruction** – the revelation of hidden or partially hidden meanings in a text. Austen set her own constraints on her intentions as a novelist, but critics have nevertheless often pointed to supposed deficiencies: there is no mention of the wars and revolutions that were the background to her life, nor of national political events; no sex or passion in stories about love and marriage. For modern critics re-reading classic texts, these perceived absences have a great significance. An extreme example of this approach may be seen in Warren Roberts's *Jane Austen and the French Revolution* (1979), in which he claims that, since Austen never mentions the momentous event, it can be identified as a brooding preoccupation in the background of her novels.

However, Angela Leighton in 'Sense and Silences' (*Sense and Sensibility and Pride and Prejudice*, ed. Clark, 1994) uses the techniques of deconstruction in her **feminist** account of the novel. Within the scope of a complex argument, she discusses the silences, the 'not-said' of the characters, particularly of Marianne, to show how the novel reveals both protest and suppression. Marianne's silences when expected to engage in the social platitudes required by society are part of her protest: the silence that surrounds her final submission to expected behaviour records her suppression:

> While for a time Marianne uses Silence as an outcry and a violation of proper speech, by the end it is used against her, to reaffirm the marginality of her place

and of her speech... Silences, in this novel, represent the protest of 'the feminine',
but also, in the end, her punishment. Jane Austen's greatness lies in the fact that,
beneath her artistic championing of Sense, she can make us *hear* those Silences
that always lie on the other side of it. (p. 65)

A MUFFLED SCREAM

In Chapter 3 of *Jane Austen* (1986), Tony Tanner identifies amid the
crucial silences 'a muffled scream' as the turning-point in Marianne's
losing battle against the constraints and secrecies of polite society. He
says that the novel characteristically 'opens with considerations of
property and concludes with the symmetries of marriage... But there is a
muffled scream from Marianne at the heart of the novel' (p. 75). This
refers to p. 154, where Marianne has received the cruel letter of rejection
from Willoughby: 'covering her face with her handkerchief, [she] almost
screamed with agony'. Tanner sees the suppressed scream as a symptom
of the sickness he believes is caused by the prevailing secrecy. There are
many secrets in the novel, from trivial sources of teasing about real or
supposed lovers, to Colonel Brandon's melancholy secret past, from
Lucy's silencing of Elinor by making a tactical confession of her secret
engagement, to Elinor's own enforced secrecy about her feelings.
Marianne herself is secretive about her courtship: her mother and sister
are unable to discover whether or not her relationship with Willoughby
has a formal basis and, Tanner says, Elinor believes that 'Marianne's love
affair should be brought out of the formlessness of feeling into the
defining forms of society' (p. 87).

In recent years, critics have been preoccupied by the novel's
juxtaposition of opposed qualities – sense/sensibility, feeling/reason,
conformity/rebellion and so on – and Austen's skill in dealing with their
ambivalence in her exquisitely **balanced** prose. Many hundreds of books
and articles have been written and continue to be written about Austen's
work: included above are a few ideas you might like to evaluate against
your own close reading of the text. As you will notice, some views will sit
fairly comfortably side by side, while others are mutually exclusive.

Finally, something of a novelty in the body of criticism is
Jane Austen and Sigmund Freud (1998) by Julian Wilmot Wynne. This
cross-disciplinary study is aware of the significance of silences in

Sense and Sensibility. Wynne also discovers some repetitions and parallels that he finds thought-provoking. First there is the precipitate disappearance of all the Dashwood girls' 'possible and impossible husbands' (Brandon, Willoughby and Edward Ferrars) in the space of a few chapters in Volume I; then there are the many 'mistaken arrivals', of which he identifies five cases: Marianne mistakes Edward on horseback for Willoughby; Mrs Jennings mistakes the Palmers' carriage for Colonel Brandon's; in London, Marianne expects a knock at the door to herald Willoughby, but it is Brandon; Elinor at Cleveland expects her mother and Brandon, but Willoughby bursts in; finally, Elinor sees a figure she believes to be that of Colonel Brandon on horseback, but it is Edward, come to propose to her. Wynne describes how 'a character – indeed the whole text of which this character is only a part – "happens" to *us*', and how in the syntax 'we almost see the character who is *not* arriving', thus keeping his presence in the novel alive.

Wynne also outlines an interesting account of the scissors-case destruction at the end of the novel, when Edward's nervous state is apparent. His behaviour is ordinarily as well as psychoanalytically understandable, but Wynne links this passage with the hair-cutting incidents earlier in the novel, relating it to Willoughby's stealing a lock of Marianne's hair, and the ring containing not Elinor's hair but that of her rival, Lucy. When he cuts the scissors-case, says Wynne, Edward is cutting his way to freedom from his earlier entanglement.

Details of the critical works mentioned may be found, with others, in Further Reading.

FURTHER READING

Jane Austen's works may be found in many editions, both hard cover and paperback. The six novels, in original order of publication, are *Sense and Sensibility, Pride and Prejudice, Mansfield Park, Emma, Persuasion* and *Northanger Abbey*. Many recent editions, including the selected text for this Note, have up-to-date commentaries in their introductions and useful notes. The authoritative editions are still those of R.W. Chapman, in Volumes I–V of *The Oxford Illustrated Jane Austen* (Oxford University Press), the most recent of which were published in the 1960s and 1970s.

Volume VI, *Minor Works,* includes Austen's **juvenilia,** early versions of her major works and unfinished work.

LETTERS

Jane Austen was a consistent and accomplished correspondent. In particular, she wrote frequently to her sister Cassandra whenever they were parted, even if only for a day or two. Unfortunately for posterity, Cassandra did her duty according to the custom of the time and censored or destroyed her sister's letters after Jane's death. What Cassandra considered unlikely to give offence remains and forms the bulk of Jane's surviving correspondence, collected and edited by R.W. Chapman in *Jane Austen's Letters* (Oxford University Press, 1932). The latest edition (1995) – also available in paperback – is edited by Deirdre Le Faye.

BIOGRAPHIES

The first account of Jane Austen's life was written by her nephew, James-Edward Austen-Leigh, and published by Bentley in 1870: *A Memoir of Jane Austen* is a discreet account of her life, with material about the Austen family gathered by her nephew and his sisters. There were many biographies published in the twentieth century, some informatively illustrated, such as Marghanita Laski's *Jane Austen and Her World* (Thames and Hudson, 1969). The most recent account, which includes some critical commentary on *Sense and Sensibility* (pp. 155–9), is Claire Tomalin's *Jane Austen: A Life* (Viking, 1997). This is a detailed account of Austen's life, which includes an analysis of some of the harsher aspects of her circumstances and the ways in which she met them.

CRITICISM

Critical writing about Jane Austen's works up until the end of the 1930s is collected and edited in Brian C. Southam's *Jane Austen: The Critical Heritage* (Routledge and Kegan Paul, 1968, 1987); Volume I covers 1811–70, and Volume II covers 1870–1938.

There is a great deal of recent commentary on Jane Austen, and particularly on *Sense and Sensibility,* which has been somewhat neglected in the past. The following brief list offers useful starting points and includes texts mentioned in this Note.

Isobel Armstrong, *Sense and Sensibility*, Penguin Critical Studies, Penguin Books, 1994

Marilyn Butler, *Jane Austen and the War of Ideas*, Oxford 1975, 1987

Robert Clark, ed., *Sense and Sensibility and Pride and Prejudice*, New Casebooks, Macmillan, 1994

David Lodge, *After Bakhtin*, Routledge, 1990

Warren Roberts, *Jane Austen and the French Revolution*, Macmillan, 1979; paperback edition, Athlone Press, 1995

Myra Stokes, *The Language of Jane Austen*, The Language of Literature Series, Macmillan, 1991

Tony Tanner, *Jane Austen*, Palgrave, 1986

Andrew Wright, *Jane Austen's Novels*, 1953, Penguin, 1962

Julian Wilmot Wynne, *Jane Austen and Sigmund Freud: An Interpretation*, Plume Publications, London, 1998

World events	Jane Austen's life	Literature
		1740 Samuel Richardson, *Pamela, or Virtue Rewarded*
		1749 Henry Fielding, *The History of Tom Jones, a Foundling*
		1755 Samuel Johnson, *A Dictionary of the English Language*
		1757 John Home, *Douglas, A Tragedy*
		1758-60 Samuel Johnson writes *The Idler* series of essays
1760 George III accedes to the throne	**1760** George Austen, Jane Austen's father, takes up trusteeship of a plantation in Antigua	
		1768 Laurence Sterne, *A Sentimental Journey Through France and Italy*
1770 Captain James Cook discovers Botany Bay, Australia		
		1771 Oliver Goldsmith, *A History of England;* Henry Mackenzie, *The Man of Feeling*
1773 The 'Boston Tea Party': workers in Boston protest against British attempts to tax the American Colonies		
1775-6 American War of Independence breaks out, following the thirteen rebel colonies' declaration of independence from Britain	**1775** Birth of Jane Austen at Steventon, Hampshire	
1777 France officially joins the Americans in the war against Britain		
		1778 Fanny Burney, *Evelina*
		1782 Fanny Burney, *Cecilia*

World events	Jane Austen's life	Literature
1783 American independence is finally recognised by Britain in the Treaty of Paris, ending the war		**1783** Hugh Blair, *Lectures on Rhetoric and Belles-Lettres*
		1784 Death of Samuel Johnson
		1785 William Cowper, *The Task*
		1786 William Beckford, *Vathek: an Arabian Tale*
1788 George III's first attack of madness		**1788** First edition of *The Times* newspaper
1789 Outbreak of the French Revolution; George Washington becomes first president of the United States of America		
	1791-2 The young Jane Austen writes *History of England* and *Lesley Castle* (for family entertainment)	**1791** James Boswell, *The Life of Johnson*
1792 France is declared a republic		**1792** William Gilpin, *Three Essays*, in which he defines the characteristics of the picturesque
1793 France declares war on Britain during the ongoing French Revolutionary Wars; execution of Louis XVI and Marie Antoinette		
		1794 Ann Radcliffe, *The Mysteries of Udolpho;* William Blake, *Songs of Innocence and Experience;* Prince Hoare, *My Grandmother*
		1796 Matthew 'Monk' Lewis, *The Monk*
	1797 *First Impressions* is rejected for publication; later rewritten as *Pride and Prejudice*	
	1797-8 An earlier work, *Elinor and Marianne*, is rewritten as **Sense and Sensibility**	

World events	Jane Austen's life	Literature
	1798-9 Jane Austen writes *Lady Susan* (unpublished; later rewritten and published as *Northanger Abbey*)	**1798** *Lovers' Vows*, an adaptation by Elizabeth Inchbald of August von Kotzebue's *Das Kind der Liebe*, first performed at Covent Garden
1800-15 The Napoleonic Wars in Europe: a continuation of the French Revolutionary Wars led by Napoleon Bonaparte		**1800** Death of William Cowper
1801 The Act of Union creating the United Kingdom of Great Britain and Ireland comes into force	**1801** George Austen retires to Bath with his wife and two daughters	
	1802 Jane Austen turns down Harris Bigg-Wither's proposal of marriage	
	1803 *Lady Susan* is bought by Crosby and Company but not published	
1805 Nelson defeats a combined French and Spanish fleet at the battle of Trafalgar	**1805** Death of George Austen; Jane Austen abandons *The Watsons*	**1805** Walter Scott, *The Lay of the Last Minstrel*
1807-8 Abolition Act outlaws Britain's slave trade		**1807** George Crabbe, *The Parish Register*, which features a character named Fanny Price
1808-14 Peninsular War in Spain between France and Britain		**1808** Johann Wolfgang von Goethe, *Faust, Part I*
	1809 Jane Austen settles at Chawton with her mother and Cassandra	**1809** First edition of the *Quarterly Review* published
1811 King George III suffers his final attack of madness	**1811** *Sense and Sensibility* published; Jane Austen starts work on *Mansfield Park*	

World events	Jane Austen's life	Literature
1812 The Prince of Wales becomes Prince Regent; Prime Minister Spencer Perceval is assassinated in the House of Commons; Luddite riots spread throughout the Midlands and the North of England		**1812** George Crabbe, *Tales*
	1813 *Pride and Prejudice* published	
1814 Allies invade France; Napoleon abdicates and retires to Elba	**1814** First publication of *Mansfield Park;* Jane Austen begins *Emma*	
1815 Napoleon escapes from Elba to march on Paris, becoming Emperor again, only to be defeated by Wellington at the battle of Waterloo	**1815** Sir Walter Scott reviews *Emma* for the *Quarterly Review*	
1815-23 John Nash builds Brighton Pavilion at the request of the Prince Regent		
	1816 *Emma* published; second edition of *Mansfield Park* appears; Henry, Jane Austen's brother, is declared bankrupt; Jane begins *Persuasion* in failing health	
	1817 Death of Jane Austen at Winchester; *Sanditon* left unfinished; *Persuasion* and *Northanger Abbey* published posthumously	**1817** Walter Scott, *Rob Roy*
		1818 Mary Shelley, *Frankenstein*
		1819 Walter Scott, *Ivanhoe*
1820 Death of George III; the Prince Regent accedes as George IV		
1833 Slavery fully abolished in Britain		
	1870 Publication of nephew James-Edward Austen-Leigh's *Memoir of Jane Austen*	

anti-jacobin term derived from the short-lived journal *The Anti-Jacobin* (1797–8), which was founded to oppose the radical views current at the end of the eighteenth century. The term is now used of literature, particularly novels, that continue this traditional approach

authorial voice the voice of the author of a literary work, wherein the reader senses interpolation by the author, which is often distinct from the voice of the narrator

balance the quality in literature of seeming rational and fair-minded; a balanced statement creates the impression of being the consequence of serious thought on the matter in question

classicism a loose term used of a variety of literary and cultural attitudes, all of which in some way look back to the conventions of Greek and Latin literature or the qualities supposed to be redolent of Greek and Roman society. The term is used in this Note to refer to those eighteenth-century writers who identified and practised 'classical' qualities, such as proportion, balance, restraint and precision of analytical reasoning

closure the sense of completeness and finality achieved by the endings of some literary works (or parts of literary works), as in the final chapter of *Sense and Sensibility* when the two heroines are married and the futures of the various characters are mapped out. The latter half of the twentieth century saw a preference for 'open' texts, which defy closure and refuse to leave the reader comfortably satisfied. By extension, it is argued that criticism should avoid closure and refuse to offer conclusive judgements, leaving the text available to multiple interpretations

comedy of manners a form of comedy much developed during the Restoration period (1660–85) and the eighteenth century: it focused on the plots and intrigues of sophisticated lovers and their circles, relying on verbal wit rather than farcical elements of comedy

deconstruction most of the ideas of the post-structuralist theory of deconstruction originate in the complex works of the French philosopher Jacques Derrida. He believes that all notions of the existence of an absolute meaning in language are wrong, yet this assumption has dominated Western thought. It should be the aim of the philosopher and critic, Derrida argues, to 'deconstruct' the philosophy and literature of the past to expose this false assumption and reveal the essential paradox at the heart of language. To 'deconstruct' a text is merely to show how texts deconstruct themselves because of this fundamental indeterminateness at the core of language. (One reason for the difficulty of Derrida's own writing is that he is aware of his own texts deconstructing themselves.) The word 'deconstruction' is now often used merely to refer to the revelation of partially hidden meanings in a text, especially those that illuminate aspects of its relationship with its social and political context. In its weakest form, 'deconstruct' has become a jargon word for 'analyse' or 'interpret'

direct speech the representation in a narrative of a character's words as they are actually supposed to be spoken, not modified by being reported; this normally requires the use of inverted commas or an alternative typographical device

discourse see free indirect speech

epistolary novel a genre of fiction in which the story is told entirely or almost entirely through letters sent by those participating in or observing the events; this was a common form for eighteenth-century novels, and one adopted, it is believed, by Jane Austen for her first version of *Sense and Sensibility*

feminism broadly speaking, a political movement claiming political power and economic equality of women with men. Feminist criticism and scholarship seek to explore and expose the masculine bias in texts and to challenge stereotypical representations of women in literature, as well as to 'recover' the many women writers and texts ignored by the male-biased canon

feminist criticism since the late 1960s, feminist theories about literature and language, and feminist interpretations of texts, have multiplied enormously. Feminist criticism is now a significant area of literary study and discussion, to the point of being a subject of study itself. A tenet of feminist thought is that male ways of perceiving and ordering are 'inscribed' into the prevailing ideology of society. This can be disclosed by studying language itself and texts in order to discover the characteristic assumptions inherent in them. In patriarchal (man-centred) societies, language contains binary oppositions of qualities, such as active/passive, adventurous/timid and reasonable/irrational, in which, it is argued, the feminine is always associated with the less 'desirable' words in the pairs listed. Women are subordinated because they are perceived through this constantly repeated framework of negative perceptions which are ingrained in language; areas of human achievement are defined in terms of male ideas and aspirations, and it is standardly presumed that advances in civilisation have always been brought about by men. Women are thus conditioned to enter society

accepting their own inferiority, and even co-operating in and approving
its perpetuation. Femininity is regarded as a construct of society.

One task of feminist criticism is to examine and re-evaluate literature in the
light of these perceptions. However, another aspect of feminist criticism involves
the study of women writers and the female imagination, sometimes known as
'gynocriticism'; this approach requires a polarisation of male and female which
can be seen as a perpetuation and tacit acceptance of the masculine/feminine
dichotomy described above

free indirect speech also known as discourse; a technique of narrating the
thoughts, decisions or speech of a character through a blend of third- and first-
person narrative; this allows an impression of access to the character's mind,
combined with a level of detachment. Jane Austen was the first major practitioner
of this technique, which has become a common means of portraying the
consciousness of characters in modern fiction

genre from the French, meaning a kind or type of art or literature. The three major
genres of literature are poetry, drama and the novel (prose), which may be
subdivided into many other genres, major and minor

Gothic novel a type of fiction that originated during the latter half of the
eighteenth century, at the same time as the general revival of an interest in the
Middle Ages. Gothic novels of this time tend to deal with cruel passions and
supernatural terrors in some medieval setting, such as a haunted castle or
monastery: famous examples include Ann Radcliffe's *The Mysteries of Udolpho*
(1794) and Matthew 'Monk' Lewis's *The Monk* (1796). Jane Austen's *Northanger
Abbey* (1818) satirises the genre. Works with a similarly obsessive, gloomy, violent
and spine-chilling atmosphere, but not necessarily with a medieval setting, are
also called 'Gothic' – Mary Shelley's *Frankenstein* (1818), for instance. Indeed,
any work concentrating on the bizarre, the macabre or aberrant psychological
states may be termed 'Gothic': thus Gothic elements are common in much fiction
up to the present day

irony a use of language, widespread in all kinds of literature and everyday speech,
which is characterised by writing or saying one thing while meaning another. Ironic
statements in literature are not always easily discerned or understood; in certain
cases, the context of an ironic comment will make clear the actual meaning
intended, but more often a writer will have to rely on the reader's shared
knowledge and values. An ironic statement on its own, therefore, is liable to

confuse anyone not familiar with the conventional attitudes implied in the work of literature in which it occurs. Jane Austen's famous opening sentence of *Pride and Prejudice* is a typical example: 'It is a truth universally acknowledged, that a single man in possession of a good fortune, must be in want of a wife.' This 'truth' (far from true and not universal) refers ironically to the fact that unmarried women want rich husbands, and that an unmarried rich man is considered a highly desirable target for their attentions. To unravel the irony, the reader is helped by knowing something of Jane Austen's society, although the novel in itself provides enough information to make the meaning clear

juvenilia the youthful works of any writer, often collected and published after death

mock heroic a term used to describe any work that treats a trivial subject with ridiculous, comic grandeur

narrative modes/narrative viewpoint a narrative is a story, tale or recital of events. To create a narrative, as distinct from a mere listing of events, is to recount a specific selection of events and establish some relationship between them. A narrative is generally composed of a mixture of different modes of writing: a novel, for instance, is likely to include dramatised incident, description, dialogue, reporting of past events, reflection by the author (and/or characters), generalised commentary and figurative writing. What brings all these elements together is the narrator. In understanding and commenting on a story, the reader's attention is immediately focused on the narrative viewpoint: What kind of connection is being made between events? Is it a carefully wrought plot or a loosely related set of episodes? How is the material being presented to an audience?

New Criticism a term used to describe a major critical movement in the United States during the 1930s and 1940s. The autonomy of literature is a vital tenet of New Criticism. A poem, for instance, must be studied (according to the New Critics) as a poem alone – not as a piece of biographical or sociological evidence, or as a demonstration of a psychological theory of literature, or for any other reason. New Criticism has had a lasting effect on critical attitudes on both sides of the Atlantic (not least because it cleared away the former amateurish historical-biographical study of literature), while developments of the 1970s and beyond have led from New Criticism to structuralism and deconstruction. However, there has been a reaction in recent years against this anti-historical critical methodology by a loose affiliation of critics, known as the New Historicists, who discuss literary works of the past in terms of their historical contexts, often minutely researched

omniscient narrator a storyteller with total, godlike knowledge of the narrative's events and characters, even to the extent of knowing the characters' innermost thoughts and motives

picturesque a term fashionable from the end of the eighteenth century, used principally in describing landscape. It complemented then-recently established aesthetic categories of the 'sublime' and the 'beautiful', and its attributes were wilderness-like qualities of roughness and irregularity. The excesses of the theory of the picturesque attracted much satirical attention, including that of Jane Austen

post-structuralism a development of structuralism, which questions the validity of structuralist theory, arguing that the signification of a text is in fact inherently unstable. The most influential post-structuralist ideas are to be found in Jacques Derrida's theory of deconstruction

realism a loose critical term used of literature (and other art) that is concerned with depicting events in a lifelike (realistic) manner. The term is used particularly of mid-nineteenth-century writing, but the attempt to portray events realistically pre-dates that period. Daniel Defoe's *Robinson Crusoe* (1719) and *Moll Flanders* (1722) are examples of works that aim to be realistic narratives, full of haphazard detail, the specificity of which is intended to imitate authentic experience. Later eighteenth-century novels composed of journals or letters, such as those of Samuel Richardson, are clearly attempts at creating a realistic narrative viewpoint, as opposed to the convention of the omniscient narrator. Jane Austen's novels brought a definitive realism to her comedies of manners, in which the events are credible, the detail of everyday genteel life closely observed and the thought and motivation of her characters lifelike. The novel took a broader view of society as the nineteenth century advanced, many writers seeing themselves as confronting and documenting new truths about people at many levels in society. Approaches to realism became a matter of constant interest to critics from then on

Romanticism this term has become so vague in general use as to be almost without meaning; however, when the 'r' is capitalised (as here), it applies to the period of English literary history from 1789 (the French Revolution) to about 1830. There are many literary interests and attributes that may be loosely labelled 'Romantic', often in opposition to those labelled 'classical' or 'neoclassical'. These include a concern to value feeling and emotion rather than the human capacity to reason; an interest in the primitive or the exotic (both geographically and historically); a conviction about the centrality of the individual; the discovery of a new relationship with nature; an appreciation of the value of imagination; and a need for rebellion against 'rules', whether of literature or society at large. The period of Romanticism covers the extent of Jane Austen's literary career, but she, of course, is an example of a writer whose interests and natural inclinations were towards the classical. As sensibility is mocked in *Sense and Sensibility*, so literary Romanticism is mocked in *Northanger Abbey*

satire literature that examines vice and folly and makes them appear ridiculous or contemptible. Satire is directed against a person or a type, and is usually morally censorious, using laughter as a means of attack rather than merely for the evocation of mirth or pleasure. However, it is a matter of critical debate whether satire ultimately serves the purpose of reinforcing rather than undermining the status quo

sensibility in general terms, the capacity to feel; more specifically, to allow literature and experience to bring forth feelings. The term can be used to define a particular type of literature popular in the eighteenth century, including the sentimental novel, which was designed to describe and evoke a tender susceptibility to feelings which later generations have often regarded as mawkish or schmaltzy. Jane Austen's *Sense and Sensibility*, of course, offers a warning about the danger of too much emotional indulgence in sensibility

sentimental novel a genre of eighteenth-century fiction which explored themes of sensibility. Such novels attempted to show that virtuous actions would be justly rewarded and that emotional affinity with the sufferings of others was proof of moral worth. Notable examples include Samuel Richardson's *Pamela, or Virtue Rewarded* (1740) and H. Mackenzie's *The Man of Feeling* (1771), or his *Julia de Roubigné* (1777)

stream of consciousness style of writing that attempts to convey all the contents of a character's mind – memory, sensory perceptions, feelings, intuitions and thoughts – in relation to the stream of experience as it passes by, often seemingly at random. This is a common narrative technique of the modern novel

structuralism a doctrine that examines aspects of human society, including language, literature and social institutions, as integrated structures or systems in which the parts have no real autonomous existence, but derive meaning and significance only from their place within the system as a whole. Structuralist critics are concerned with language in general and, more broadly, all conventions and codes of communication. Structuralism has now been superseded by more radical post-structuralist theories, in particular deconstruction

subtext the underlying, implicit situation or purpose that can be discerned in the behaviour of characters or the narration of events in a literary work, but which is not referred to explicitly and which may never be fully explained

symbolism the use of symbols in a work of literature or other art. A symbol is something that represents something else by analogy or association – a writer may use conventional symbols that form part of a literary or cultural tradition, as well as creating new ones. The application of Freudian psychoanalysis sometimes finds symbolism of which the author was unaware

tone the words an author chooses in a literary work may impart a particular mood, or dictate the manner in which a sentence should be read: angrily, imploringly, monotonously, pompously, wittily, and so on. Tone is thus a critical concept which implies that literature is like speech, requiring a speaker and listener; tone is the attitude adopted by the speaker towards the listener, and may be gathered and understood from the kind of syntax and vocabulary used. To achieve full understanding of a work, it is essential to recognise its tone(s)

voice a term used in a semi-technical sense to denote the persona in a narrative, i.e. 'the person who is narrating'. The word 'voice' thus reminds us that the basic relationship between narrator and reader is like hearing an individual speaking; the reader decides what that person is like, understands what tone is being used and thus discerns the narrator's attitude to the story being told

Author of this note

Delia Dick was one of the first Open University graduates; her postgraduate study was at the University of Warwick, where she currently teaches English literature. She is also the author of York Notes on Daniel Defoe's *Moll Flanders* and Jane Austen's *Mansfield Park*, as well as Alan Bennett's *Talking Heads*.

NOTES

Notes